"PLAYING IN THE HOLE"

This edition published in 2008

Copyright © Carlton Books Limited 2008

Carlton Books Limited
20 Mortimer Street
London W1T 3JW

A CIP catalogue record for this book is available from the
British Library

ISBN: 978-1-84732-144-2

Editor: Martin Corteel
Designer: Jake Davis
Project Art Editor: Paul Chattaway
Production: Lisa Cook

The publishers would like to thank the following sources for their
kind permission to reproduce the pictures in this book.

All photography **Carlton Books** except the following:

iStockphoto: /Fabio Bustamante: 6, 60; /Dave Lewis: 4b, 83, 102,
107, 111, 123, 157, 172, 184, 216, 234

Every effort has been made to acknowledge correctly and contact
the source and/or copyright holder of each picture and Carlton
Books Limited apologises for any unintentional errors or omissions,
which will be corrected in future editions of this book.

Printed in Great Britain

"PLAYING IN THE HOLE"

Compiled by
Adrian Clarke & Iain Spragg

with a foreword by **Matt Le Tissier**

CARLTON

CONTENTS

FOREWORD

Foot-in-mouth disease is as much part of our beautiful game as shin pads, yellow cards and half-time oranges.

Whether it's an adrenaline-fuelled player in a post-match interview, an overexcited commentator or a tongue-tied pundit, we've all dropped the odd verbal clanger and this book celebrates football's finest and funniest faux pas.

Anyone brave (or stupid) enough to stand before the dreaded microphone and share their thoughts with the world is just one unfortunate slip of the tongue away from disaster and embarrassment. No one, it seems, is immune. If they were, this book wouldn't exist.

I hope you enjoy this collection of the game's hilarious gaffes, blunders and clangers. And don't forget, it's when the final whistle blows and the talking starts that things gets really interesting.

Best wishes,

Matt Le Tissier
May 2008

INTRODUCTION

As the old saying goes, footballers like to let their feet do the talking, and judging by this brand spanking new collection of metaphor-mangling, tongue-twisting verbal volleys, it's an adage they should certainly stick to.

Let's face facts, those associated with the beautiful game aren't exactly renowned for their eloquence. Even the professionals behind the microphone are prone to the curse of "foot-in-mouth" disease that seems to strike down the great and the good, and with virtually every new interview, post-match press conference and tirade, a classic clanger is added to the collection.

If they weren't, this would be the shortest book since Arsène Wenger started writing "Incidents I have Actually Seen on the Pitch".

So we hope you enjoy this trawl through football's funniest faux pas, linguistic lapses and commentary catastrophes. To paraphrase the immortal words of Kevin Keegan, "We'd luv it, really luv it" if you did.

Adrian Clarke & Iain Spragg
May 2008

I M THE
BOSS

"In the supermarket you have class one, two or class three eggs and some are more expensive than others and some give you better omelettes. So when the class one eggs are in Waitrose and you cannot go there, you have a problem."

Apparently Jose Mourinho would never shop in Tesco

"I've learned that you have to score goals to win games."

Rafa Benitez is nothing if not a tactical genius

"I think I must have run over six black cats since I've been at Wolves."

The RSPCA wants a word with Wolves boss Glenn Hoddle

"We've had the snow this week, so we've done very little training. We've built an igloo and had a snowball fight, so we might have to put the balls away in future and take the players to a snowdome instead."
Aidy Boothroyd reveals Watford's revolutionary training techniques

"Up front we played like world beaters – at the back it was more like panel beaters."
Paul Jewell doesn't rate the Wigan defence then

"The good thing about these early kick-offs is that you can go out for a meal and still be all in your pyjamas for half eight."
Neil Warnock likes his early nights

"Ricardo has worked with me for four years and I do not understand these quotes, he probably needs to see a doctor."

Jose Mourinho wants a word with Ricardo Carvalho

"It's up to the fans to help me now. If they see any member of my squad in a pub, club, bar, whatever, I want them to ring me up and tell me. If my players want to drink they can get pissed in the safety of their own homes."

Warnock favours a tipple indoors

"It's like having a blanket that is too small for the bed. You pull the blanket up to keep your chest warm and your feet stick out. I cannot buy a bigger blanket because the supermarket is closed. But the blanket is made of cashmere."

Jose Mourinho stretches his supermarket analogy to breaking point

"Today's game is a 30-pointer."
Billy Davies gets a little carried away

"The match for them is a bit like people down south going to the theatre. They want to be entertained."
Kevin Keegan highlights the great north-south divide

"He really is special. If he runs at you, you're in trouble. He'll do 14 stepovers and give you twisted blood."
Harry Redknapp on Cristiano Ronaldo

"If you want to sleep, you don't become a football manager."
Steve Coppell suffers from insomnia

"We develop players. We don't have them growing in greenhouses out the back because we don't have time for greenhouses. We're more of a microwave sort of club."
Aidy Boothroyd wants quick results

"I'm not an electrician, even though I'm known as 'Sparky'. But I was hoping the lights would stay off."
Mark Hughes welcomes a floodlight failure at Upton Park

"I couldn't be more chuffed if I were a badger at the start of the mating season."
Ian Holloway – student of amorous animals

"The only way we will be getting to Europe is on Easyjet in the summertime!"
Steve Coppell plays down expectations

"If I were a fisherman, I would never think I'm not going to catch a single fish."

Gerard Houllier is an optimistic angler

"I know what is around the corner – I just don't know where the corner is."

The genius of Kevin Keegan

"Manchester United defended with great spirit and a lot of effort and their future is only looking better for them now. But they are not good enough to be champions, only to finish closer to us and not drop quite so many points."

Jose Mourinho heaps faint praise on United

"He has that smell to be where he needs to be at the decisive moment. When there is chocolate to take in the box, he is there."
Arsene Wenger reckons Julio Baptista knows a thing or two about Quality Street

"Was it as good as sex? Probably, yeah. It's a long while since I've had sex – you'd have to ask the wife."
Iain Dowie reveals a little too much after Coventry snatch a late equaliser

"I was excited and it takes a lot to get me excited... ask my wife!"
...As does Roy Keane

"It wasn't a monkey on my back, it was Planet of the Apes!"
Mick McCarthy's classic primate pun

"I banned the players from stuffing their faces with chocolate. On the bus, the players chanted 'we want our chocolate bars'."

Arsene Wenger could have a riot on his hands

"I cannot put into words just how much promotion means to me but if I could I would put it in a can so I could open it later."

Reading boss Steve Coppell feels like celebrating promotion with a few cans

"The challenge on Robbie Savage has been brushed under the table."

There must a shortage of carpets chez Mark Hughes

"Hopefully we can go to Arsenal and keep a clean sheet. But it will be very difficult. Anything can happen at Highbury. Maybe hundreds of squirrels will come on to the pitch and we will have a problem. You cannot prepare for things like that. We will probably have to run from them."
Martin Jol is preparing for anything ahead of the north London derby

"He wears a suit, so he's a tactician. He wears a tracksuit, so he's a motivator. He carries a clipboard, so he's a bus conductor."
Stuart Pearce on the many talents of Rafa Benitez

"I've got too many Cavaliers in my side and not enough Roundheads. Too many players with plumes and feathers but not enough hard workers. And the Roundheads won in the end."
Paul Sturrock loves his history

"Is he entitled to go dance with his wife at a do? Yes he is. Does he need some help with his dance moves? Obviously he does. We will do some more movement to music in training."

Palace boss Iain Dowie leaps to Andrew Johnson's defence

"It just came in so quickly, he tried to get a head on it but it came off the wrong corner of his head."

Nigel Worthington has too many square-headed players

"I would love to say the goal was well rehearsed on the training ground, but we've not been there for three weeks because it has been flooded."

Steve Bruce is nothing if not honest

"I could have another moan but I'm sick to death of my own whingeing."
Steve Bruce decides to keep quiet

"It was awful. Sometimes you have one or two players who are not doing their job, but on this occasion we had about a dozen."
Maths was never Sven-Goran Eriksson's strong point

"I watched Arsenal in the Champions League the other week, playing some of the best football I've ever seen, and yet they couldn't have scored in a brothel with two grand in their pockets."
Ian Holloway reckons the Gunners are firing blanks

"Apparently he was eating a lasagne and somehow pulled a hamstring – it has to be a world first."

Micky Adams is mystified by his injury list

"It's a bit strange if you're a player to see remarks on the TV but there's no problem with Jermain. After the story, I told him I wouldn't swap him for Miss World – he would probably swap me for Miss World though."

Martin Jol fancies Jermain Defoe

"My family are really happy here at Liverpool and I am prepared to have my daughter with a Scouse accent, even though it is sometimes a problem for me."

Rafa Benitez is prepared to make big sacrifices to stay on Merseyside

"When I hear them say they can win the title it makes me feel like laughing."

Jose Mourinho doesn't rate Liverpool's title chances then

"We are like the primary school boys walking into the secondary school for the first time and finding out who the bully boys are."

Derby boss Billy Davies rolls with the blows after promotion to the Premier League

"Sadly, I have been unable to persuade FIFA, UEFA and the Premier League to allow me to use 12 players in every game."

Rafa Benitez thinks Liverpool deserve special favours

"If it was a boxing match, it would be Muhammad Ali against Jimmy Krankie."
Fight fan Aidy Boothroyd reflects on Watford's defeat to Manchester United

"When you are in a dogfight, you have to fight like dogs. If it is a gunfight, you can't afford to go in with just a knife."
Chris Coleman fancies a fight

"I said to my wife, 'come on, it's Valentine's Night, I will take you out somewhere special'. So I took her to Brentford against Southend."
Alan Curbishley is an old romantic really

"They have my credit card number and we will say, 'How much do you need this week? Let's do it.'"
Arsene Wenger loves his trips to face the FA's disciplinary panel

"We went to watch a Billy Joel show. Half of the foreign lads weren't quite sure who Billy Joel was, but I enjoyed it anyway. For the Charlton game I'll really punish them – I'll take them to see Mamma Mia."

It's tough playing for Harry Redknapp...

"Young players are a little bit like melons. Only when you open and taste the melon are you 100% sure that the melon is good. Sometimes you have beautiful melons, but they don't taste very good and some other melons are a bit ugly and when you open them, the taste is fantastic."

Jose Mourinho gets fruity

"You can compare us at the moment to a bit of soft porn – there is an awful lot of foreplay and not a lot going on in the box."

Rochdale manager Keith Hill wants more "action"

"I don't read the papers, I don't gamble, I don't even know what day it is!"
Steve McClaren confirms what we all suspected

"Seriously, the boy glides across the park. If he walked across a puddle, he wouldn't make a splash."
Harry Redknapp thinks Theo Walcott is the Messiah

"This transfer window should not be allowed. Us managers can only buy all our shopping in four weeks and just imagine if that was the case for Christmas shopping. You can imagine the queues."
Maybe Ian Holloway should buy new players online

"He reminds me of a hunting dog. When I want something specific done, he is very willing to learn."

Rafa Benitez sings Jamie Carragher's canine praises

"Steven Gerrard had his house burgled last week but we were robbed in broad daylight here."

Brian Laws shows his sympathetic side after Sheffield Wednesday lose to Palace

"All the restaurants were full and we couldn't get in, so we celebrated with a takeaway kebab instead."

Neil Warnock treats his players to a doner and chips

"If we win, we go to the semi-final. If we lose, I will go to Earls Court and watch the wrestling on the 24th with my children."

Jose Mourinho plans ahead

"He had so much space you could have put a bungalow in there for his retirement."
Mick McCarthy wants the Wolves defence to tighten up

"I have seen the film The Alamo and right now I feel like I've got Davy Crockett behind me. Sometimes I feel like I could put my head in a bucket of water."
Stuart Pearce needs to cool down

"We were pumping in crosses when we should have been cuddling the ball."
Tactile tactics from Alan Curbishley

"It's a long time since I've seen a player who you feel would kick his granny to win, and that's lovely – though not for the granny."
Glenn Roeder has bad news for Steven Taylor's family

"For me it's been a good season, but we've only made a cake. Now we need to put the cherry on top."

Next season Rafa Benitez will buy the candles

"It's like a marriage. You want to do things in life but if you don't have anyone to share it with, then it's not as fulfilling."

Gareth Southgate sends an SOS to Middlesbrough's AWOL fans

"If we are going to go Americanized, we are going to have all these girls waving things every time there is a goal. You ask them to run up and down in Sheffield with very little clothing on – it would be hard work for them."

Neil Warnock isn't keen on unnecessary razzmatazz

"Look at my haircut. I am ready for the war."
**Jose Mourinho idolised Action Man as
a kid**

"Despite the global warming, England is still
not warm enough for him."
**Arsene Wenger bids a fondish farewell to
Spaniard Jose Reyes**

"If a haulage company wanted a new lorry
and someone said in September you cannot
have one until January, it would not be
allowed."
**Gary Megson is worried about truck
supplies**

"I think we won that game against Liverpool
because we scored and they didn't."
Nothing gets past Jose Mourinho

"People said I was pitting my wits against Sir Alex Ferguson but it is like using a water pistol to take on a machine gun."
Steve Bruce on Birmingham's defeat at Old Trafford

"Football is all about winning, drawing and losing."
Peter Taylor covers the bases

"When you have an argument with your missus, you know when you're ready to go back and talk to her. You leave her alone for a bit because you know if you talk to her she will bite your head off. That's what life's about – and it's the same with footballers."
Tony Mowbray on his West Brom squad

"Not only have they taken my arms and legs, now they've cut my balls off."
Dennis Wise can't believe the FA after they docked Leeds 15 points

"That was like a Bond film where the villain has so many chances to kill him off, doesn't take them and eventually he comes back to bite them."
Lawrie Sanchez prefers a clean kill

"I had problems at first, confusing 'wine' and 'win' and my players would laugh."
Rafa Benitez has his Liverpool squad in stitches

"If they are naive and pure, then I'm Little Red Riding Hood."
Rafa Benitez isn't fooled by Arsenal

"Jens changed his mind but wasn't quick enough to respond to his brain."
Arsene Wenger on Jens Lehmann's two heads

"Mansfield gave us one hell of a game. I feared extra time but we are still on the march, still unbeaten, and I'm still a brilliant manager!"

Harry Redknapp loves himself

"At the moment we've only got 16 first-team players and my initials stand for Mick McCarthy, not Merlin the Magician."

McCarthy just can't conjure up any more bodies

"I'm not prone to outlandish predictions but this club can establish itself in the top eight of the Premier League."

Paul Jewell has big ambitions for Derby. Sort of.

"Once Ashley [Young] puts some weight on he will be fantastic. At the moment he's about three-and-a-half stone – a couple of times we have put him through the letterbox."
Martin O'Neill likes to post his players

"It was just handcuffs at dawn."
Alex Ferguson mixes his metaphors

"When we meet in airports we don't fight."
Apparently, Arsene Wenger likes to fight Alex Ferguson elsewhere

"I don't think we'll be professional for the full 90 minutes until the microchips are firmly imbedded in the players' heads."
Aidy Boothroyd has ground-breaking plans for his squad

"I was a young lad when I was growing up."
Nothing gets past David O'Leary

"It's about time us managers had a fight. I wouldn't be daft enough to have a go at Sam Allardyce but me and Bryan Robson would be decent. I'd have to kill him or he'd keep coming back at me!"

Steve Bruce has radical plans to liven up football

"At the moment, things are not going for us. We'd probably need a dog to run on the pitch to head it into the net for us."

Aidy Boothroyd isn't fussy where the goals come from

"Arsenal didn't have one single chance, including the goal."

Avram Grant and his rose-tinted spectacles

"Get hit in the bollocks, get hit in the nose, the gob, knock your crowns out. I'm not bothered but do not let it spin into the top corner."
Mick McCarthy favours physical defending

"I've just seen the replay again for the first time."
David Moyes is caught in a time loop

"When I was Walsall's manager, I didn't know you had to coach and train players."
Management came as a shock to Paul Merson

"It's just a game of football. There are 1.2 billion people in India who couldn't give a shit what happens to Reading."
You can't say Steve Coppell doesn't have a sense of perspective...

"I was never tempted to become a punk. I was Sidney Serious, I was into George Benson. I was smooth. Smooth as a cashmere codpiece."
Ian Holloway, anti-punk

"The best finishers are those strikers who don't care how many they miss."
Glenn Hoddle on the art of scoring goals

"Even the chef's been out for two weeks with a hernia."
Alan Curbishley laments West Ham's injury crisis

"I liked to ski-jump, but I couldn't out-jump Eddie The Eagle – he was special."
Sven-Goran Eriksson reveals his unusual sporting hero

"If we're not careful, we will be playing in high heels and skirts and playing netball."
Steve Bruce yearns for the days of football's true hardmen

"Emre has a left foot that can open a can of peas."
Alex McLeish reckons the Turk is packing a Swiss Army Knife

"They searched the house and took a computer away that I bought my wife two years ago – I think she learnt to turn it on four weeks ago."
Harry Redknapp's missus needs IT advice

"People say we are having no luck, but we are – it's just all bad."
Gareth Southgate refuses to lose his sense of humour

"If you ask if I'd rather see Chelsea or Man United win the title, then I will answer Arsenal."

Nul points for Arsene Wenger

"Some of our top players are out injured. That's an excuse, but it's also not an excuse."

Wigan boss Chris Hutchings just can't make his mind up

"The problem was conceding four goals in the first half."

Rafa Benitez was happy with the second 45 minutes

"I am sure we will see pictures of Sam [Allardyce] in his Speedos walking along a beach somewhere. That won't be a pretty sight."

Steve Bruce sums up the feelings of the nation after Allardyce is sacked by Newcastle

"My players travel more than Phileas Fogg in Around The World In 80 Days. Javier Mascherano had to play a friendly for Argentina in Australia. That must have been really important."
Rafa Benitez wants to keep the Air Miles down

"By the time you read this we'll have had a scan on Fabregas. His foot blew up after the game and that's not the best sign."
Arsene Wenger on Fabregas's "explosive" foot

"I don't think my wife would be naked with anyone – she hardly ever gets naked with me. And with a face like mine, I don't blame her."
Ian Holloway knows he's no Brad Pitt

"I said it in pre-season. In fact, I may have said it before the season started."
Sir Alex Ferguson's logic: impeccable

"I'm pleased for Georgios [Samaras]. He can be a handful on any given day and trip over the ball on any given day."
Stuart Pearce offers distinctly qualified support for his player

"I saw Danny Mills and Robbie Savage lying next to each other, comparing tattoos – they seemed like lovers."
Paul Jewell reveals just how close his Derby players really are

"The crowd were dead. It was like a funeral out there."
Sir Alex Ferguson wants the Old Trafford faithful to liven up a bit

"I bought a Sade CD the other day and after listening to it for a while, I thought, 'Christ, no wonder she isn't famous any more'."
Ian Holloway, music critic

"He's just training here but we're well equipped to handle it. We have everything that's needed, including mirror doors."
Arsene Wenger can't wait for David Beckham to join the Gunners in training

"When we lost, I used to have so much trouble sleeping that I became addicted to Night Nurse. When I told my wife, she thought I was talking about some bird in suspenders."
Harry Redknapp on the medicinal wonders of cough medicine

"My confidence is 100 per cent in Frank Lampard but I told him if the next penalty is at a key point then it's better for another player to take the responsibility."
Jose Mourinho leaps to his player's defence

"It's the same if you told my wife I'm gay. A big laugh."
Martin Jol cracks himself up

"I'm not jumping on the Andy Johnson for England bandwagon – I'm driving it."
Iain Dowie has his hands on the wheel

"The only way we will get into Europe is by ferry."
Kevin Keegan plans Newcastle's team bonding trip

"There was one point where I am sure
Richard Dunne thought he was Maradona."
**Sven-Goran Eriksson likes to brainwash
his players**

"People tell me he hasn't scored in open play
for 11 months but he shouldn't force things.
Maybe he has got to think about that a wee
bit and then the chance will come. One might
hit him on the backside and go in the net to
start things off for him."
**Alex McLeish bemoans Gary
McSheffrey's bum deal**

"I hated Robbie Savage when he played
against me. He is one of those characters
you despise when he is playing for the
opposition, but you love when he is on your
team."
**Paul Jewell's love-hate relationship with
the Wales midfielder**

"I don't know if you know but with the football kit today there are no pockets. Nobody can put their hands in their pockets."
Avram Grant has no idea where modern players keep their spare change

"Trust me, I'm comfortable not being pals with people."
Roy "Cuddly" Keane

"I pinned the poem, 'If', by Rudyard Kipling, up in the dressing room but I don't think any of the players could make head or tail of it. I left it up for an hour but took it down before it got defaced."
Mike Newell thwarts Luton's graffiti artists

"I would love an Aston Martin but if you ask me £1 million for an Aston Martin, I tell you, you are crazy because they cost £250,000."
Jose Mourinho knows his motors

"The wife told me it looked as if I knew what I was doing a bit more."
Gareth Southgate trades in his tracksuit for a suit

"It looked like we'd picked 11 people off the streets and asked them if they fancied a game."
Steve Bruce isn't impressed

"Fail to prepare, prepare to fail."
Roy Keane, football poet

"It's no good having money in the bank and no good players out on the pitch."
Tony Mowbray is desperate to splash the cash

"Somebody's just given me a video of the game. I don't know why they handed it to me because there's no way I'm going to watch that again."
Neil Warnock won't torture himself any more

"Whenever a ball came towards them, it was like a bouncing bomb."
Steve Bruce witnesses an explosive encounter

"[Anthony] Stokes could be a top, top player in four or five years or he could be playing non-league."
Roy Keane hedges his bets

"If they don't want to come because their wife wants to go shopping in London, it's a sad state of affairs."
Roy Keane bemoans WAG power

"We were good friends until we started winning, then he started changing his mind."
Rafa Benitez falls out of love with Jose Mourinho

"I think the haircut helps. Having my hair cut used to help me. I used to feel leaner and sharper. Meaner. So I might shave mine next month."
Roy Keane plans his next haircut

"The only feedback I've had off the chairman is him asking me 'do you want a pie'?"
Steve Bruce settles in at Wigan

"I would love to gather all the fans together to say goodbye but they would crush me with their love."
Jose Mourinho's ego threatens to get out of hand

"I've got more points on my licence – I'm not joking!"

Derby boss Paul Jewell on his side's meagre points haul

"Brian Clough kept my feet on the ground. Like when he punched me after a game for making a back pass."

Roy Keane relives the old days

"I've got to choose my words carefully but I thought the supporters let us down badly today. We needed them for the full 90 minutes today and we didn't get that. And, for me, that's a disgrace."

Norwich manager Peter Grant endears himself to the crowd

"I don't predict in football. All I predict is next week against Barnsley you will see a vastly different Norwich City team."

Glenn "I'm not Nostradamus" Roeder

"That's it with Owen – you shoot holes in him and he comes back for more."
Kevin Keegan, sharp shooter

"There are some guys who have this big telescope to look into the homes of other people and see what is happening. Wenger must be one of them and it is a sickness."
Jose Mourinho accuses the Arsenal manager of voyeurism

"Working with people on a field turns me on."
Graeme Souness has an outdoor fetish

"If you buy a man who is half-dead, everybody may be happy off the field, but on the field you'll have major problems."
Arsene Wenger likes his players alive and kicking

"I'm not going to make it a target, but it's something to aim for."

Steve Coppell has nothing in particular in his sights then

"You can play chess for about 10 hours and still lose, know what I mean?"

Sir Alex Ferguson, Grand Master

"The lad got over-excited when he saw the whites of the goalpost's eyes."

Steve Coppell gets over-excited in his post-match press conference

"The owner told me he wants to be in Europe within 18 months. Whether that means we're all going to Majorca next summer, I don't know."

Neil Warnock dusts off his passport

"I just thought 'sod it, let's just attack them'!"
**Steve Coppell reveals his in-depth
tactics**

"I think there was just a little change today
and I started to smell that things were
improving a little bit."
**David Moyes has a good nose for
the game**

"I'm not someone to fear things. They say in
Holland 'have no fear, Jolly is here!'"
Martin Jol is scary back home

"Our major problem is that we don't know
how to play football."
Sam Allardyce hits the nail on the head

"I've slept with a coat hanger in my mouth to keep the smile on my face these last couple of days."
Mick McCarthy has been having sleepless nights

"If I made a mistake then I apologise. I am happy that I'm not going to jail because of that."
Jose Mourinho doesn't want to do time

"He is flat out in the dressing room – I just knocked him out. Now I might go round and burn down his house."
Wolves boss Dave Jones on his "special" relationship with his former player Chris Marsden

"The only decisions I'm making at the moment are whether I have tea, coffee, toast or cornflakes in the morning."
Sam Allardyce takes things easy after being sacked by Newcastle in 2008

"Footballers are totally pampered. Apparently, the ridges on some of the team socks are quite uncomfortable."
Ian Holloway thinks modern players need toughening up

"I don't predict in football. All I predict is that next week you'll see a vastly different Norwich team."
Glenn 'Mystic' Roeder

"I'm not looking for excuses but another 24 hours would have been nice to have prepared for the game. But that's about the only excuse if I'm looking for excuses, which I'm not, but it was a factor."
Wrexham boss Brian Little doesn't want to play the blame game

"There are a load of tarts playing the game who fall down at the drop of a hat."
Mick McCarthy wishes players would keep their headwear firmly in place

"I'm 110 per cent committed to this club and you can't get more committed than that."
Kevin Keegan never does things half-heartedly

"At this time of the season you get to see people like oranges – you squeeze them and some of them tend to capitulate."
Watford boss Aidy Boothroyd prefers firm fruit

"It was like watching paint dry – it was rubbish."
Derby boss Paul Jewell tells it like it is

"I didn't see the incident as a penalty, although I haven't seen it."
Alan Curbishley should go to Specsavers

"We've got six games left – two at home and three away."
Chris Coleman's 'sixth sense' deserts him

"If you took the goals out of it, I think it was pretty even."

Alan Curbishley stays positive after West Ham's 4–0 hammering against Chelsea

"I should invite you sometimes to come into the dressing room and look at the legs of Alex Hleb after a game. You would be amazed."

Arsene Wenger is a great admirer of his players' pins...

"We're playing our usual away formation. A bloke up front who can't run and two wide men who don't track back."

Harry Redknapp tries to lull the opposition into a false sense of security.

"It's like a child, sometimes you have to give them a sweet, when they are bad you have to shout at them."

Juande Ramos wants a crèche at White Hart Lane

"Nothing was different to other games. What was different was we lost."

Nothing gets past Chelsea's Avram Grant

"Football is like fighting a gorilla – you don't stop when you're tired, you can only stop when the gorilla is tired."

Chris Coleman has been watching too many Tarzan films

MEN IN BLACK

"The referee made three mistakes only. The red card, playing too much time at the end of the first half and the penalty. Apart from that he was good."

Avram Grant isn't one to criticise officials

"The problem with officials is that sometimes they get too officious."

There's just no pleasing Andy Gray

"We'll see you in the second half for the next part of the Uriah Rennie show."

Preston's half-time announcer isn't impressed with Mr Rennie

"We were robbed. That is the second time this season that referee has ruined a game for me. He spoilt the night. I am almost speechless."

George Boateng, not quite speechless

"The officials were the worst team tonight. They were indecisive throughout and there was practically manslaughter on James Scowcroft."

Neil Warnock loses his sense of perspective

"I was surprised first of all that I was sent off for what I said. It's like if the speed limit is 60mph – sometimes you are not caught when you drive 70mph and sometimes you are caught when you drive 61mph. I drove 60.5mph."

Arsene Wenger is banished to the stands

"Referees aren't looking at what they should be looking at. You need to prioritise. It seems the main issue this season is whether three or four Chelsea players surround referees, or say things they shouldn't say."

Avram Grant feels the pressure

"We asked the fourth official to tell the referee to stop the game and take away the balloons – or kill them."
Sven-Goran Eriksson really hates parties

"You only have to fart in the box to concede a penalty these days."
Kevin Blackwell smells a conspiracy

"Those decisions cost us three points and possibly £50m. Dowd by name, Dowd by nature. The only thing consistent about these fellas is their inconsistency."
Paul Jewell won't be sending Phil Dowd a Christmas card this year

"Because you're Australian and you always beat us at everything."
David Elleray explains his decision to book an Australian player

"We had Phil Dowd at Arsenal last year and we were denied three stonewall penalties so maybe he has it in his Premier League contract that he doesn't give away penalties against Arsenal."
Paul Jewell expands on a theme

"Once apon a time, if you told people you were from Tring they'd say 'Oh yeah, that's where Walter Rothschild is from'. Now they say 'That's where that bloody referee lives."
Graham Poll puts Tring on the map

"I know Rob Styles. He will get up in the morning, look in the mirror and wonder how the other seven wonders of the world got on."
Ray Houghton reckons referees are getting vainer

"Some referees don't like it. They don't like the truth. But I just told him how bad he was in the first half."
Sir Alex Ferguson exchanges pleasantries with Mark Clattenburg

"In Italy the referees are all handsome and athletic. Here, they have tubby little bellies."
QPR owner Flavio Briatore has a crush on Continental officials

"We have got the drug testers here today. They shouldn't be going to see the players – they should go to see the officials instead."
Mick McCarthy advocates a zero tolerance policy

"The penalty – I have to choose my words very carefully – it was a disgrace."
Robbie Keane tells it like it is

"He gave the penalty and then he pointed the other way. It's a disgrace. I don't know what he sent me off for – I wasn't listening. Walking on the pitch perhaps?"
Dennis Wise is distinctly unimpressed

"It is difficult to lose the game on a wrong decision. It was offside and it is proven on TV. Why do we have to take it? I still don't think it's right. We have to do something about it. Yes, I am angry."
Arsene Wenger is definitely not happy

"Thank heavens the official is an intimate friend of mine. I talk with the referee all the time. We speak together regularly and, when we are able, we dine together."
Barcelona boss Frank Rijkaard teases Chelsea rival Jose Mourinho

"They call themselves professional. They're not professional. Professional means you're good."
Paul Jewell, a fan of amateur officials

"Are the rules you can go first for the man when the ball is in the air and everybody decides it's not a foul, or do we make it a judo party and maybe everybody will be happy?"
Arsene Wenger again, still not satisfied

"Even the referee shook my hand. He could have given me a penalty – that would have been even better!"
Alan Shearer is a hard man to please

"It's almost impossible for referees these days – they need eyes in the back of their heads which they haven't got."
Graham Taylor took biology GCSE

"I think they just want the referee to blow up at this point."
Martin O'Neill sums up everyone's feelings

"Newcastle are a good team, like Everton. At Everton, there are 30,000 referees, in Newcastle there are 50,000."
Jose Mourinho sees referees everywhere

"I don't know if the referee was wearing a Barcelona shirt because they kicked me all over the place. If the referee did not want us to win, he should have said so from the off."
Thierry Henry suspects favouritism

"Rooney was complaining all the time, protests and more protests. He reminded me of my kids."
World Cup official Horacio Elizondo

"We had a referee who, in my opinion, wasn't up to the required standard and that isn't bleating about the referee."
Burnley boss Steve Cotterill is definitely, absolutely not complaining

"Mark Halsey didn't have a decision to make, apart from giving the penalty."
Chris Kamara can't quite make his mind up

"There is no question their goalkeeper conned the referee. His action forced the referee to book Cristiano. Why would he want to go down? He was on a hat-trick, he had gone round the keeper and he was brought down. It was a ridiculous decision."
Sir Alex Ferguson is outraged

"I just think the FA are inherently weak when it comes to these issues. We've been eroding the power of the referee for years and years. I've been refereeing in the Premiership since 1993, I'm the most experienced referee they've got and yet my credibility no longer holds."
Graham Poll lets rip

"McCarthy shakes his head in agreement with the referee."
Martin Tyler is no body language expert

"I know referees have a difficult job to do and he's not helped by the antics of a striker who's thrown himself around for most of the
match. He was on the floor more than he was standing up."
A rare moment of empathy for officials from Steve Bruce

"If the referee stands by that decision, I have two wooden legs. I will be seeing this ref again in my dreams – and I won't be kissing him."
Ian Holloway has nightmares about the match officials

"I thought Michael Johnson should have had a penalty but the referee booked him for filming."
Sven-Goran Eriksson should have told his players to leave their camcorders in the dressing room

"Rafa is trying to get the referee on his side. He must think we are bloody stupid."
Sir Alex Ferguson wants referee Steve Bennett all too himself

"I've got to be very careful with that I say about the referee because I thought he was poor all game really."
Middlesbrough's Luke Young fails to hold his tongue

"The official has got his hand on Joe Jordan's backside."
Commentator Alan Green exposes the seedy side of match day refereeing

"As for the fourth official, he is a doughnut."
And Bolton boss Gary Megson reckons the referee is a Danish pastry

"We had two different referees. In the first half he was laid back and let things go. In the second half he was a terror."
Steve Coppell reckons Mark Clattenburg is football's answer to Jekyll and Hyde

FAN
FRENZY

"Who's the midget in the suit?"
West Ham fans salute vertically-challenged
Bolton boss Sammy Lee

"He's big, he's Scouse, he looks like Mickey
Mouse – it's Franny Jeffers, Franny Jeffers!"
**Sheffield Wednesday fans salute their
club's new signing**

"Just one Capello, give him to me, delicious
manager, from Italy!"
**England fans welcome the new boss at
Wembley**

"He's bald, he's old, he never plays in
goal – Jens Lehmann, Jens Lehmann."
**Arsenal's goalkeeper gets a warm
welcome at the City of Manchester
Stadium**

"We sing better than your wife."

The DC United crowd let David Beckham know they're not Spice Girls fans

"What's that coming out of the air? It's Martin Laursen, it's Martin Laursen."

Aston Villa fans love their Danish defender

"One Lily Savage, there's only one Lily Savage."

Arsenal fans to Blackburn's Robbie Savage

"Mourinho are you listening, you'd better keep our trophy glistening, because we'll be back in May to take it away, walking in a Fergie Wonderland!"

Manchester United fans want the title back at Old Trafford

"We're not fickle. We just don't like you."
Aston Villa supporters get their message across to David O'Leary

"Stevie Gerrard, Gerrard, he kisses the badge on his chest then puts in a transfer request, Stevie Gerrard, Gerrard."
Manchester United supporters question the Liverpool star's loyalty

"He's big, he's Red, his feet hang out his bed, Peter Crouch, Peter Crouch."
Anfield pays homage...

"He's big, he's tall, he's clumsy on the ball – Peter Crouch."
...As do the Everton fans

"He's fat, he's round, he's kicked us out our ground, Robbie Williams, Robbie Williams."
Scotland fans make their feelings clear after the pop star's concert at Hampden forces them to move to Parkhead

"You're going home in a combine harvester."
Stevenage fans taunt their Exeter counterparts

"He comes from Zimbabwe, he'll score eventually!"
Portsmouth supporters serenade striker Benjani

"We hate the English more than you."
Republic of Ireland and Germany fans find something in common

"You're just a fat Spanish waiter."

Bolton fans welcome Liverpool manager Rafa Benitez...

"It's neat, it's weird, it's Rafa's goatee beard!"

...As do the Liverpool supporters

"If you made a lot of money selling biscuits, buy our club."

West Ham fans welcome new owner – biscuit baron Eggert Magnusson

"We're gonna deep fry yer tapas!"

Aberdeen fans make themselves at home in Madrid

"Dichio, Dichio, Danny Dichio, he's got no hair but we don't care, Danny Dichio!"

Preston fans love their follically-challenged striker

"Sit down potato head!"

The West Brom faithful taunt Birmingham boss Steve Bruce

"There's only one Jimmy Krankie!"

Leeds boss Dennis Wise enjoys a warm welcome at Molineux

"You're just a fat Eddie Murphy!"

Arsenal fans to Jimmy Floyd Hasselbaink

"One Song, we've only got one Song!"

Charlton supporters salute Alexandre Song

"You only sing when you're fishing!"

Hull City's away support endear themselves at Grimsby

"He's fat, he's round, he bounces all around, Sammy Lee, Sammy Lee."

The Bolton boss is a firm favourite at Stamford Bridge

"He's got no hair, but we don't care, Martin, Martin, Jol".

Spurs fans salute their Dutch boss

"Yousef's here and Yousef's there, here we go, Moroccan all over the world."

Norwich supporters to Yousef Safri

"Whinge on the telly, he's going to whinge on the telly!"

Middlesbrough fans taunt Bolton boss Sam Allardyce

"Beaten by a franchise, you're getting beaten by a franchise."
MK Dons fans love their history

"If you hate Bryan Robson, throw your shoes!"
Sheffield United fans aren't exactly enamoured by their manager

CUP
CHAOS

"If we win, we go to the semi-final. If we lose, I will go to Earl's Court and watch the wrestling on the 24th."
Jose Mourinho has his bases covered ahead of Chelsea's Champions League quarter-final

"We are not going to win the FA Cup and I do not care less about it, to be honest."
Reading's Dave Kitson does his bit for the FA Cup

"We were down at a corner in front of The Kop when they were singing 'You'll Never Walk Alone'. I was standing next to Gerrard and singing along with them. He looked at me like I was a weirdo!"
Havant & Waterlooville's Jamie Collins enjoys his side's FA Cup clash at Anfield

"It doesn't matter what happened in the game – we got the three points."
Wayne Bridge fails to grasp the concept of the Carling Cup final

"I dreamed about scoring in the FA cup as a kid. Trust me to have my thunder stolen by a few balloons."
Luton Shelton reflects on his bizarre goal for Sheffield United, courtesy of a deflection off a stray balloon

"I've never had a good record in the FA Cup – apart from winning it."
Gary McAllister is his own harshest critic

"I'm sure sex wouldn't be so rewarding as this World Cup. It's not that sex isn't good but the World Cup is every four years and sex is not."
Brazil's Ronaldo is obviously at it all the time

"Really I'd want to win everything, whether it's a cup competition or the Premier League or the UEFA Cup."

Spurs boss Juande Ramos fails to understand the UEFA Cup format

"The Cup with the big ears is the holy grail to me. It starts the child in me dreaming."

Claude Makelele gets religious thinking about the Champions League trophy

"It's a good advert for the cricket season."

Mark Lawrenson isn't impressed by the FA Cup final

"The Liverpool players are passing the cup down the line like a newborn baby. Although when they are back in the dressing room they will probably fill it with champagne, something you should never do to a baby."

Alan Parry dishes out invaluable parenting advice

"I got Carragher's shirt and he signed it. We had talked about putting all the shirts in a draw but when you get a shirt like that, it ain't going in no draw."

Rocky Baptiste forgets his team-mates after Havant & Waterlooville's FA Cup clash with Liverpool

"We went for a walk before the game and a bird dumped right on my head. They say that can be a lucky omen – and it was!"

Barnsley manager Simon Davey after his side's shock FA Cup win at Anfield

"Everyone seems to think we will be the victims of an FA Cup upset – but then again I've been second favourite for the sack all season!"

Gareth Southgate hasn't lost his sense of humour

"If [Rafael Benitez] wants me to stay on my feet, maybe he should tell his defenders to stop hitting me."
Didier Drogba ramps up the tension ahead of Chelsea's Champions League semi-final with Liverpool

"I wouldn't put my house on it. I've worked too hard over 35 years to get a house."
Gordon Strachan isn't exactly brimming with confidence ahead of Celtic's Champions League showdown with Barcelona

"Although Barcelona are the favourites, there aren't any teams that stand out as favourites."
Glenn Hoddle can't quite decide who to back in the 2007–08 Champions League

"I have had a drink with them in the dressing room – even though you cannot tell. It's quite a nice diet and sometimes it lets them eat and drink totally out of control – and yes, that includes champagne."

Juande Ramos shows his players how to party after their Carling Cup final triumph

"I know what it's going to be in the next round – us against Chelsea. I'm going down to Soho Square to check those balls."

Sir Alex Ferguson cast aspersions on the FA Cup draw

"If I play them in the Champions League, I want to go there and kill them – that's my message."

Jose Mourinho is still full of love for Chelsea after quitting Stamford Bridge

MICROPHONE MADNESS

"He looks like a man who has nits and worms at the same time."
Mark Lawrenson's worrying diagnosis of Aston Villa boss Martin O'Neill

"Scotland can't afford to take their minds off the gas."
Andy Townsend on the Tartan Army's mental fuel

"By trying to sign Peter Crouch, are Middlesbrough aiming too high?"
Jeff Stelling, stand-up comedian

"It's like the Sea of Galilee – the two defenders just parted."
Mark Lawrenson gets all Biblical

"We did wonder about the possibility of a Spurs versus Tottenham draw."
Matt Smith does his best to confuse the ITV audience

"There is a no-smoking policy in all parts of the Layer Road ground. Anyone who is caught smoking will be taken away, strapped to an electric chair and electrocuted until they are dead. Thank you."
The Colchester stadium announcer makes his point

"There's a certain Englishness about the English game."
Fair comment from Alan Parry

"He's multi-lingual. He'll say 'ouch' in five different languages."
Mark Lawrenson on cunning linguist Philippe Senderos

"That free-kick was so wide it nearly hit my car."
Paul Merson is worried about his no-claims bonus

"Spurs did well in the first half, closing Tottenham down."
Spurs man-marked themselves, according Robbie Earle

"Pinpoint accuracy from Beckham there. Two inches lower and it would've been a goal."
Gerry Armstrong needs a tape measure

"Murphy was unselfish, but I feel he should have shot himself."
David Pleat is a tad harsh

"Nothing surprises me in football, nothing – but this is a bit of a surprise!"
Tommy Docherty loses the plot on Radio Manchester

"Stamford Bridge holds 42,000, so 10 per cent of that would be about 4.1 thousand."
Mike Parry's calculator goes on the blink

"Both the keepers are suffering from confidence."
Alan Shearer likes nervous goalkeepers

"A bit of pushing and shoving between Deco and Sissoko. It's like a terrier picking a fight with an Alsatian, but in this instance the terrier comes out on top as the Alsatian is booked. Obviously dogs don't get yellow cards in the park."

The BBC's Charlie Henderson unravels a canine conundrum

"You can't turn a sow's ear into a rose. Or a flower."

Mike Parry mixes his metaphors

"The one thing Cristiano Ronaldo has is pace, quick feet and a great eye for goal."

Chris Waddle has more than one thing on his mind

"They've scored 32 goals in every game this season."
Alan Parry heaps a little too much praise on Arsenal

"The next match here at the Banks's Stadium is on New Year's Day, which this year falls on January 1st."
The Walsall PA leaves nothing to chance

"Martin Jol is literally a dead man walking."
Steve Claridge thinks the Spurs boss is a zombie

"You feel for Chimbonda there. It's come off the post so fast it's in slow motion."
Eagle-eyed Glenn Hoddle

"Reina's name in Spanish means queen – and he came out like a queen there and kicked it straight at his defender."
The PC era has clearly passed Gerry Armstrong by

"At Hearts there's just a few seconds left. One thousand, four hundred and forty seconds in fact, because they kicked off late."
Jeff Stelling is a stickler for accuracy

"And here comes Crouch, like some sort of rampaging super spider."
Peter Drury has a dark imagination

"Prica has scored for Sunderland – his dad is rumoured to be called Pap."
Ian Payne spices up his commentary

"Ronaldo got into the area and had about 11 legovers."
Paul Merson on the United star's "scoring" habits

"As the old saying goes, people in glasses shouldn't throw stones."
Because they might not hit the target?
Alan Smith (Snr)

"The top four sides will always be the top four sides."
Andy Gray doesn't predict big changes in the future

"Most managers would give their right arm for a European Cup, and Paisley had three."
The BBC's Manish Bhasin on the three-armed Liverpool icon

"He didn't have his body behind that one but luckily he has arms like an orang-utan."
Stuart Lovell makes a monkey of Hibs goalkeeper Yves Kalambay

"And the score is nil-nil, just as it was at the beginning of the game."
Mike Ingham has been keeping an eye on the scoreboard

"Tottenham haven't created many chances. Robbie Keane's flashed a couple of times but nothing more."
Andy Gray cops an unwanted eyeful

"Peter Schmeichel will be a father figure for Kasper."
Jamie Redknapp states the alarmingly obvious

"Liverpool are going to have to start getting results if they're going to start winning."
Andy Townsend has wise words for the Reds

"He was a dead man walking...he didn't have a leg to stand on."
Five Live's Malcolm Boyden ties himself in metaphorical knots

"The team colours of both these sides need no introduction. Tottenham are in white and Chelsea are in blue."
John Motson quickly changes his mind

"You can only score against the team you're playing against."
David Platt, tactical genius

"I see they are wearing the white of Real Madrid – that's like a red rag to a bull."
Is David Pleat colour-blind?

"He's a typical winger in that he's not brave and tackling's not a strong point – although he's not afraid to go into a tackle."
Les Ferdinand reckons Ashley Young has a split personality

"Only Arsenal have scored more goals than Arsenal this season."
Dicky Davies can't get the Gunners off his mind

"The alarm bells are flashing."
Rob Hawthorne witnesses a sound and light spectacular

"In this league, any team can beat any other – and to prove it there were seven draws yesterday."
Don Goodman's theory falls distinctly flat

"There's only one person who knows how he missed that, and that's Wayne Rooney, and even he doesn't know."
George Graham searches for answers

"Riise's had four chances. I wouldn't say two of them were chances, mind."
Andy Gray confuses himself

"If Arsenal lose now, I'll eat my heart."
Craig Burley is nothing if not confident watching the Gunners take on Reading

"I think they'll have to throw the kitchen sink at them now a bit. Maybe not the whole sink, with all the plumbing – maybe just the taps for now."
David Pleat urges caution

"A handball is when your hand touches the ball."

Gary Lineker answers the question no-one was asking

"Reading just had a great five-man move that involved everyone."

Phil Thompson's figures just don't add up

"He should have been given the goal of the season for that shot, even though it went wide."

Pat Nevin fails to grasp the whole "goal of the season" concept

"If there is a qualified referee in the ground, please can he make himself known to a steward."

The waggish Fulham half-time announcer isn't impressed with the referee's performance

"Adebayor was queerly frustrated."

Does Jeff Stelling know something we don't?

"Avram Grant literally is in a no-win situation – unless he wins."

Graham Taylor offers hope to the Chelsea boss

"He had it on a plate, he had the sausage, bacon and eggs on it as well, but he couldn't take it."
Chris Kamara makes a meal of his breakfast analogy

"Today will live with them for the rest of their lives. Well, at least through the summer."
Jamie Redknapp dramatically shortens footballers' life expectancy

"Arsene Wenger uses the FA Cup to bleed his youngsters."
It's tough being an Arsenal youngster, according to Alvin Martin

"Diouf is a master of the dark art of the winger. He draws you in, then he sucks you off."
Garry Birtles appears to be on intimate terms with El-Hadji Diouf

"Of course, Steven Gerrard is one of only a few Liverpool players who never gets left out by Rafa. And even he doesn't always get picked."
David Pleat reflects on Benitez's rotation policy

"Man United's defensive record is second to none... apart from Liverpool's that is."
Warren Barton gets his back fours confused

"Late goals come in short bursts and Sunderland's burst has gone on for a long time."
Phil Thompson on the Black Cats' staying power

"The amount that Chelsea have missed Petr Cech can't be overplayed – although Jose Mourinho has overplayed it."
Peter Beagrie can't quite make his mind up

"David Moyes does like to get dirty with his players."
Team bonding at Everton, according to Charlie Nicholas

"Today I'm joined by Paul Walsh who won the Cup with Spurs in 1991, Phil Thompson who won it in 1974, Paul Merson who won it in 1993 and Matt Le Tissier. What are you doing here?"
Jeff Stelling puts the boot in on Soccer Saturday

"Parkin's making a run towards the box, he might get there sometime this week."
Jonathan Pearce doesn't rate Jon Parkin's pace then

"A memorable half hour to forget!"
Alan McInally is in two minds about the first 30 minutes

"They are fourth in the Championship, and you can't ask for more than that."
Mark Bright aims low

"We all thought West Ham were dead and buried when they lost 4–3 to West Ham."
Jamie Redknapp on a very local derby

"If you keep walking past the barbers, eventually you'll get a haircut."
Paul Merson muses on Middlesbrough's relegation prospects

"Marseille needed to score first and that never looked likely once Liverpool had taken the lead."
Nothing gets past David Pleat

"Scholes walks away a bit gingerly."
David Pleat states the insultingly obvious

"I understand why Paul Jewell took the Derby job, but I just wonder why he went there."
Phil Thompson was thinking of the "other" Derby job

"I'm not saying we shouldn't have a foreign manager, but I think he should definitely be English."

Paul Merson wants an Anglo-English England manager

"Diouf's got more previous than Jack the Ripper."

Colin Murray pays the Bolton striker the ultimate compliment

"Liverpool were all mishy-mashy. I know that isn't a word, but it should be."

Paul Merson, a modern-day Doctor Johnson

"Michael Dawson clearly put his ball to the hand."

What game is Iain Dowie watching?

"If United don't equalise, they might lose this game."
Micky Thomas cuts to the chase

"They'll have to literally have eyes in the back of their heads."
Jamie Redknapp wants mutant players

"Theo Walcott is carrying a nation, literally, on his shoulders."
Andy Townsend reckons Walcott is some sort of Charles Atlas

"Arsene would've thought in the past, 'Thierry will get me 20, Pires 15, Ljungberg 12.' That's 50 goals."
George Graham failed GCSE maths

"Anelka used to have days where he'd seem to have got up on the wrong side of the bed. Maybe Sam's pushed it up against the wall so he can only get out on the good side."
Paul Merson lifts the lid on Sam Allardyce's innovative management techniques

"And here's Jose Mourinho talking to the Chelsea manager Garth Crooks."
Stamford Bridge role reversal courtesy of 5 Live's Spoony

"What will you do when you leave football, Jack – will you stay in football?"
Stuart Hall, broadcasting genius

"Nobody is Didier Drogba."
Phil Thompson on Chelsea's non-existent striker

"If Malbranque's early chance had gone in, we'd have a completely different scoreline."
Alan Green is definitely keeping count

"Alan McInally never broke a metatarsal in his career. Matt Le Tissier never broke sweat in his."
Jeff Stelling sticks the boot in again

"Is the way Rooney and Tevez play off the cuff or just as it happens?"
Geoff Shreeves answers his own question

"Arsene Wenger built a stadium at Arsenal, though he didn't actually build a stadium."
Tony Gale is the architect of his own downfall

"David Unsworth is fatter than me and Gavin Mahon couldn't even pass wind accurately today."
Commentator Martin Price is thrilled with his visit to Vicarage Road

"Steven Gerrard was Liverpool's only senior player tonight. Well, OK, they had two: Hyypia, Gerrard, Fowler and Dudek. So that's four."

Jamie Redknapp gets there in the end

"I'd compare him to the incomparable George Best."

David Pleat on the one and only Cristiano Ronaldo

"We want zero-tolerance on players sliding in, but sometimes you have to let one or two go."

Chris Kamara is prepared to bend the rules

"If they released a Titus Bramble bloopers DVD, it would be four hours long."

Adrian Chiles twists the knife

"He looks like a fish up a tree – out of his depth."
Confusion reigns for Paul Merson

"Ballack is having a nightmare. They'll be changing his name soon."
Chris Waddle, cunning linguist

"The opening ceremony was good, although I missed it."
You've got to admire Graeme Le Saux's honesty

"Don't hoover up while Chelsea are playing because if you knock the telly, Robben will fall over."
Ruud Gullit thinks Robben is a soft touch

"Terrible marking, you don't mark open spaces. Open space has never scored a goal in a football match."
Steve McMahon isn't impressed with the defence

"Everton have not won without being in the lead."
Andy Gray sums up the Merseyside derby

"It's not easy on the eye but it's super to watch."
Steve Claridge has double vision

"Matt Taylor is off – and what a chance he had. Two chances – three in fact, actually, if you count the third."
Gary Weaver can't make his mind up

"Steven Reid's knee has blown up, so we've sent him back to Blackburn."

Ray Houghton reflects on an explosive tackle

"Milan Baros isn't the greatest-looking of players."

Jamie "Handsome" Redknapp doesn't fancy Villa's striker

"Fuller scored Stoke's penalty, putting it in the wrong corner."

There's just no pleasing John Solako...

"When you get injured at 20, it's not a problem because you're fit."

Phil Thompson fails to grasp the concept of "injured"

"When you concede two goals, you've got to score three to win a game."

Peter Reid's sums are impeccable

"The defender was so laid back there he was almost vertical."

Frank Stapleton loses his bearings

"They have to concentrate not only when they have the ball or when their opponents have the ball, but also when neither of them has the ball."

Graham Taylor covers all the bases

"I used to think my name was 'Stop The Cross', I heard it so much."

Lee Dixon has an identity crisis

"Ian Pearce has limped off with what looks like a shoulder injury."

Tony Cottee failed his medical exams

"When you're walking onto a bus and trying to get there before the person in front of you, that's a different level of competition to playing in front of 80,000 people."

Graeme Le Saux never gets a seat on the 8:15

"I was inbred into the game by my father."

David Pleat reveals a disturbing family secret

"If Plan A fails, they could always revert to Plan A."

Mark Lawrenson doesn't like teams changing tactics

"This game is, I think, what my children would describe as 'pants'."
Gary Lineker makes presenting look like child's play

"It was that game that put the Everton ship back on the road."
Alan Green, all at sea

"Tugay is writhing all over the place as if he were dead."
Alan Green has been watching too many zombie films

"A tremendous free kick. It probably would have gone in if he had put it where he intended to put it."
Stan Collymore's a stickler for accuracy

"I was saying the other day how often the most vulnerable area for goalies is between their legs."

Andy Gray, anatomy expert

"It looks like he's got a bit of a knock there, judging by the language on his face."

The player's face speaks volumes, according to Clive Tyldsley

"Nervy, edgy, cautious – a bit like Alan Hansen on the dancefloor."

Gary Lineker puts the boot in

"They say football is unscripted drama and this match certainly hasn't followed the script tonight."

Conor McNamara loses the plot

"In the bottom nine positions of the league
there are nine teams."
Ray Stubbs' sums are impeccable

"Chris Porter scored his first league goal last
week, and he's done the same this week."
**Jeff Stelling experiences a strong sense
of déjà vu**

"Football's football. If that weren't the case, it
wouldn't be the game that it is."
It's hard to argue with Garth Crooks

"It's one of the greatest goals ever, but I'm surprised that people are talking about it being the goal of the season."
Andy Gray can't quite make his mind up

"The club has literally exploded."
Ian Wright gets a tad carried away

"The penalty was as clear as night is day."
Alan Green doesn't know what time it is

"It was against Chelsea that Peter Crouch had that giraffe-on-acid moment."
Jeff Stelling let his imagination run wild

"Nicolas Anelka is so physically strong, he's not unlike Anelka."
Jamie Redknapp thinks the French striker has a twin

"When you're down, you Palace fans, the fickle finger of fate rarely smiles on you."
Jonathan Pearce mixes his metaphors

"You've got to take the rough with the smooth. It's like love and hate, war and peace, all that bollocks."
Ian "Mr Sensitive" Wright

"You talk about captaincy and leadership, that's no captaincy. He's acting like it's the last day of the season and they've lost the title. I played for managers that would be turning in their graves. He's the captain!"
Alan Hansen disapproves of William Gallas's histrionic reaction to Arsenal's 2–2 draw away to Birmingham City (23 February 2008)

"For Manchester United to get back into this game, it will be a tall order against a tall side who are well ordered."
Martin Tyler spells it out

"They've got a teletepathic, teletepathic, pathetic, well it's not pathetic... oh just forget it."
Graham Taylor suffers a severe case of foot in mouth disease live on air

"Tugay ran the midfield with absolutely no legs."
Stan Collymore thinks athletes are overrated

"An embarrassing defeat tends to more harm than good."
Chris Kamara's logic is impeccable if blindingly obvious

"They say they're the best side in the world but Barcelona are not on top of Serie A, are they?"
Tim Lovejoy failed his geography GCSE

"Newcastle defender Steven Taylor was dancing all over the place like a teapot."
Mark Lawrenson knows something about teapots that the rest of us don't

"I'd have put my house on Adebayor scoring. If I had one."
Paul Merson needs a roof over his head

"Man United aren't so much a team as a group of players."
Nothing escapes David Platt's beady eye

NORTH OF THE BORDER

"You people sometimes are like those serial killers you see in films who send out these horrible messages. The serial killer who cuts out the words 'I am going to get you' or 'your wife is next'. You are the very same."

Celtic boss Gordon Strachan is a big fan of the Scottish media

"We'll stay in a very nice hotel, travel up on a nice bus and in the morning we'll have a nice walk."

Mark McGhee is big on life's niceties

"I can't count the number of times I've seen him being literally invisible tonight."

Archie MacPherson on the vanishing prowess of Celtic's Shunsuke Nakamura

"We're in football to play in big games. And games don't come any bigger than the semi-final of the Cup at Hampden."

John Collins doesn't rate Hibs' chances of making the final

"Craig Beattie's an important player for us. He's quick, he's very fast, and he's got great pace."

Scotland manager Alex McLeish reckons Beattie's a bit sharp then

"We're bottom of the league, but it's only a third into the season – not even halfway."

Dunfermline boss Stephen Kenny knows his maths

"If you can manage Celtic, you can be Prime Minister."

Gordon Strachan has political ambitions

"We hate Coca-Cola, we hate Fanta too, because we're the Tartan Army and we love Irn Bru!"

Scotland fans are very particular about what they drink

"This is not a reality check for us because we never thought we were Brazil."

Christian Dailly reflects on Scotland's defeat to Belarus

"I don't know if Alex McLeish knows whether I'm Scottish or not. Maybe I'll have to put 'Mac' in front of my surname."

Colchester striker Chris Iwelumo really, really wants to play for Scotland

"I said to them last week that I'd like them to win ugly and they certainly won ugly today. That was the ugliest thing I've seen since the ugly sisters fell out the ugly tree."
Motherwell boss Terry Butcher isn't big on the beautiful game

"Alan Hansen might be bigger than me, but when you come from Glasgow that doesn't matter. Whether he's 6ft 6ins, it doesn't matter in Glasgow. It doesn't matter because once I chop his legs off, we'll be the same height."
Billy Davies doesn't see eye-to-eye with Alan Hansen

"I never divide up the bearskin before the bear is shot."
Hearts chairman Vladimir Romanov is a cautious hunter

"I have done everything in my career but this will be new and different."

Terry Butcher joins the Scotland national set-up

"As you know, China is a communist state and you have to conform. Owen is a non-conformist. I gave him a copy of Das Kapital and he thought it was a guide to the capital cities of the world."

Dunfermline boss Stephen Kenny sings Owen Morrison's praises

"I thought it was a bit high – he nearly took my willy off. You would probably expect that from Bob but there you go."

Inverness' Ross Tokely is a forgiving soul

"Just like 17 per cent of us have ginger hair, a lot of us Scots are small. You could build up a hugely talented Celtic side and Snow White would have to lead them out because there are so many small people here."

Gordon Strachan "bigs up" the Bhoys

"If it's a game of football, Rangers will lose."

Pundit Fraser Wishart reckons Rangers should stick to rugby

"He's taking over at the worst time, because Scotland are sitting so proudly at the top of their group. There's only one way they can go – they can either stay there or go the other way."

Craig Brown reckons Alex McLeish is facing a downhill challenge

"I beg you Mowgli, take the monkeys back to the Safari Park."

Hearts chief Vladimir Romanov reveals to the press he's a big Jungle Book fan

"I am Scotland manager until something else happens."

Alex McLeish is a firm believer in fate

"John Hartson is the laziest player I've seen. When you look at him you can easily see he needs some exercise."

Celtic goalkeeper Artur Boruc on how to build team spirit

"We're the famous Tartan Army and we're here to save the snail."

Scotland fans on a culinary crusade in Paris

"All the cul-de-sacs are closed for Scotland."
Joe Jordan sees road blocks everywhere

"Ryan O'Leary had to come on in the second half because Simon Ford was feeling his groin at half-time."
Kilmarnock boss Jim Jeffries explains his substitution

"The world looks a totally different place after two wins. I can even enjoy watching Blind Date or laugh at Noel's House Party."
Gordon Strachan is clearly losing his marbles

"If I had my hair, I'd be pulling it out."
Dundee boss Alex Rae remembers the good times

"At his age, he is not going to play forever."
**Scotland boss George Burley signals
David Weir's international retirement**

"We have scored 101 goals this season.
Not bad considering we don't play with any
strikers."
**Walter Smith hits back at critics of his
Rangers side**

"They had a dozen corners, maybe 12 – I'm
guessing."
It's a good job Craig Brown isn't a baker

"All the cul-de-sacs are closed for Scotland."
Joe Jordan yearns for the open road

"We'll have more football later. Meanwhile, here are the highlights from the Scottish Cup final."
Gary Newbon proably won't be holidaying north of the border this summer

"The Pope is not a bad lad. If he said 'God bless Myra Hindley', I might have a problem."
Gordon Strachan gives the Vatican an equivocal thumbs up

"This is the best night of my career – apart from missing the penalty."
Rangers skipper Barry Ferguson focuses on the positives after his side's Uefa Cup semi-final triumph

"Neil Lennon wasn't sent off for scoring a goal, and that's what annoys me."
There's just no pleasing Martin O'Neill

"I don't want to sound homophobic but I want a Scottish manager."
Pat Nevin confuses his phobias

"I don't know the Scottish players and I really don't know much about Scottish football."
Fiorentina's Alessandro Gamberini hasn't really done his homework ahead of his side's showdown with Rangers

"There's only one Nakamura, one Nakamura, He eats chow mein and votes Sinn Féin, Walking in a Naka wonderland."
Celtic supporters' pay tribute to their Japanese midfielder

"If Livingstone don't keep their discipline the inevitable could happen."
Mark Hateley dusts off his crystal ball

"I predicted in August that Celtic would reach the final. On the eve of that final I stand by that prediction."
Archie MacPherson is wise before and after the event

"Venegoor just turns and lampoons it into the net."
Toomy Smyth reveals the satirical bent of Celtic's Dutch striker

"If I was to declare an interest in this job the Tartan Army would string me up."
Scotland boss Alex McLeish doesn't want the vacant Birmingham job – for four months at least!

INTERNATIONAL DUTY

"I think I'd be brilliant! My ego thinks I'd be brilliant. Actually the rest of me thinks I'd do it brilliantly!"

Martin O'Neill reckons he could do the England job

"Guus Hiddink is lucky. He has a horseshoe as big as my house."

Ruud Gullit on Australia's "fortunate" coach

"It was a sense of numbness really – how the hell are we out of this World Cup? It even got to the point where there were weird ideas – maybe if we'd had brown rice rather than white."

Rio Ferdinand clutches at straws after England's 2006 World Cup exit

"Romania are more Portuguese than German."

Barry Venison needs a map...

"The Brazilians were South American, but the Ukrainians will be more European."
...but Phil Neville doesn't

"I lament the score. I'm sorry for Colombia and for my country. We dominated the game."
Colombia coach Jorge Luis Pinto after his side's 5–0 defeat to Paraguay

"Football is not played on paper, it is played on a pitch. This game is not mathematics and in football, two plus two very rarely equals four – it's usually three or five."
Trinidad & Tobago coach Leo Beenhakker reveals why so many footballers fail their maths GCSEs

"If you put an 'o' on the end of his name, then he is going to be good, isn't he?"
Paul Jewell isn't convinced Fabio Capello is the right man for England

"The Belgians will play like their fellow Scandinavians, Denmark and Sweden."
Andy Townsend relocates Brussels

"The fans who want to see Messi, Tevez, Saviola and Aguero all together should go out and rent Snow White and the Seven Dwarfs."
Argentina FA boss Julio Grondona likes big players then

"Sven's a lucky man with the ladies. In fact, he's very lucky because, with respect, he's no Brad Pitt."
Martin O'Neill obviously doesn't fancy the former England boss

"The good news for Nigeria is that they're two-nil down very early in the game."
Kevin Keegan is an optimist

"It was nice to get the first session out of the way and get a bit of a feel for each other."
Steven Gerrard on England's tactile training sessions

"I don't think you can blame a player for missing a penalty. I don't think we missed a penalty individually, I think we missed it collectively."
Stuart Pearce defends his Under-21 charges en masse

"For a game played in Cologne, that stunk."
It's the way Mark Lawrenson tells 'em

"My granny could probably have managed Brazil to World Cup success."
Gary Lineker doesn't rate "Big Phil" Scolari

"I've got the passion but no idea of tactics – I'd be like a black Kevin Keegan."
Ian Wright stakes his claim for the England job

"There's more chance of me flying Concorde to the moon blindfolded than there is of you taking Wales to the South African World Cup."
Robbie Savage's word of encouragement for Wales boss John Toshack

"I enjoy playing against the big men and I will just have to get the stepladder out and get on with it."
Wales' James Collins looks forward to marking 6ft 7in Czech Republic striker Jan Koller

"To be the England manager you must win every game, not do anything in your private life and hopefully not earn too much money."

Sven-Goran Eriksson knows a thing or two about international management

"Zidane can decide a game. When the ball goes to his feet it doesn't cry – when it goes to my feet it cries."

Perhaps "Big Phil" Scolari should change his socks

"I watched a bit of the England game then turned over and watched a Victoria Beckham documentary instead."

Steve Coppell isn't impressed with the Three Lions

"Big Kyle is full of energy, he'd chase paper on a windy day."

Billy Hamilton on Northern Ireland's irrepressible Kyle Lafferty

"I would walk back from the United States to play for England again."
David Beckham doesn't mind getting his feet wet

"It's about putting square pegs into square holes."
Steve McClaren sums up his England philosophy

"Why do you go for a foreign guy? It is like you go to war and say 'Now we choose a general from Portugal or a general from Italy'. Would that cross your mind? Never."
Arsene Wenger is perplexed by Fabio Capello's appointment as England manager

"This is a young group and sometimes I don't like some of the things I see. Here we are with another five-star hotel, overlooking the sea at Rimini. So if the waves are making too much noise in the evening, just phone down and we will try to move you to a room on the other side."

Wales boss John Toshack thinks his players are a little too pampered

"It was a very professional performance, but the second half was totally unprofessional."

Kevin Radcliffe on a game of two halves for Wales

"Scotland were like a dog with a bone and when they got the bone, they made it count."

Charlie Nicholas admires Scotland's tenacity

"I feel like a man who has given the double of his key to a mate. The guy comes, takes your car, uses it for 10 days and leaves it in the middle of a field without any petrol."

Arsene Wenger on the perils of players going away on international duty

"Sven was top-drawer and I really liked him. He was straight and honest – even if he did look like Mr Burns from The Simpsons."

David James sums up the feelings of a nation

"England do not have a game until February, so why make a decision over a bacon butty at 8.30am?"

Sir Alex Ferguson on the FA's early-morning decision to axe Steve McClaren

"I'm like milk. Once it's gone past its expiry date you can't drink it anymore."

Spain coach Luis Aragones isn't sour

"There are no easy games in international football, but I'll go as far as to say that this is one of them."

Craig Bellamy tempts fate

"The England fans have sat and watched for the first half... now they're giving them the clap."

Graham Taylor on the dubious habits of the Three Lions supporters

"This team has some of the best players in England."

David Beckham assesses the strengths of the England team

"My players travel more than Phileas Fogg in Around The World In 80 Days. Javier Mascherano had to play a friendly for Argentina in Australia. That must have been really important."

Liverpool boss Rafa Benitez is a massive fan of international football

"We knew at half-time we were only half-way there."

Wales skipper Simon Davies knows exactly how long a match lasts

"It was a funny one. It was one of them ones that either goes in, or goes over the stand – and as I say, it was neither."

Northern Ireland striker Warren Feeney hedges his bets

"England should've won against Croatia because they had 800 million people in the stadium."
Sky's Alan McInally reflects on a world-record attendance for an international match

"We respect them for the good players that they are but at the end of the day if you have to kick them, you kick them."
Kenny Miller reveals Scotland's no-nonsense tactics

"The England job is an impossible job. Particularly for an Englishman, it's tougher than being Prime Minister."
Glenn Hoddle, who knows a thing or two about the FA hot seat

"I said right at the start I would live and die by results and results haven't gone my way. In that sense we have failed."

Steve McClaren chooses his words carefully

"Watching the Premier League is like Formula One – it's that quick – and then you go to an international game and it's like a game of chess."

Robert Green wants England to get into second gear

"I've always said that Iraq is the Brazil of the Middle East. We have beautiful skill in this country, we have treasures walking on the ground that we must develop, not just below the ground in the form of oil."

Iraqi coach Sadiq al-Wohali thinks his players are priceless

"I think it's the worst job in football."
Neil Warnock doesn't want the England job then

"It was good just to see them train, get a feel of them."
George Burley gets tactile with the Scotland squad

"You always lose when your opponents score and you don't."
France coach Raymond Domenech is nobody's fool

"It was much too intellectual for a footballer to have written it. The spelling and punctuation were all correct."
Curtis Davies reveals how he learned of his England call-up

"I am happy for the fans to chant Beckham's name. He is a very good player and I know him well. But those songs don't influence me at all."

Fabio Capello isn't a music fan

"I am not a Messiah."

Fabio Capello plays down expectations

"We were in an awkward position against Yugoslavia, in that in order to win we needed to score more goals then they did."

Spanish coach Jose Antonio Camacho feels sorry for himself

"The Belgian team were just standing around looking at each other, and that's no remedy for success."

Chris Waddle teaches English as a second language

"The Czech Republic are coming from behind in more than one way now."
John Motson's unfortunate double entendre

"The one thing England have got is spirit, resolve, grit and determination."
Alan Hansen gets carried away

"I've never eaten anyone so there is no reason anyone should be scared of me."
Fabio Capello definitely isn't Hannibal Lecter

"You'll have to get on your knees and beg before I play for you again."
Nicolas Anelka wants France boss Jacques Santini to say sorry

"I'm happy with my language progress – the only difficulty when I tour Premier League matches is that different people talk to me in different accents – and sometimes I can hardly understand a word."
England boss Fabio Capello reflects on his visit to Anfield

"It was a successful failure."
Kenny Miller paints Scotland's failed Euro 2008 qualifying campaign in a positive light

"There's a real international flavour to the World Cup."
Jimmy Armfield gets to the heart of the matter

"You always lose when your opponents score and you don't."
France coach Raymond Domenech believes football is a simple game

"We knew at half-time we were only halfway there."

Wales Simon Davies likes to go for the full 90 minutes

"The Scotland team changes coach? Who is the Scotland coach now?"

Lithuania boss Algimantas Liubinskas has his finger on the pulse ahead of his side's European Championship qualifier

"Zidane can decide a game. When the ball goes to his feet it doesn't cry – when it goes to my feet it cries."

Maybe Portugal boss Phil Scolari needs to change his socks...

"We are super happy! We have to deliver ourselves to God and on the day God was Portuguese."

Portugal goalkeeper Ricardo is grateful for a spot of divine intervention

PLAYER POWER

"Sometimes on a day off I go to the Krispy Kreme doughnut shop. When we play at home, I go there after the game and it's like a doughnut party! Everyone is eating doughnuts inside their cars – it's like a disco!"
Arsenal's Cesc Fabregas knows how to party

"I prefer to frighten people by driving around in my white Porsche with Slipknot blaring out of the windows."
Reading goalkeeper Marcus Hahnemann loves Halloween

"We played like a bunch of drunks."
Yossi Benayoun hammers West Ham's performance

"It's disappointing to be dropped from any team – even my mates' fantasy league team."
Robert Green hates sitting on the bench

"When I see Almunia's performances, I get
angry and have to make a fist in my pocket."
Anger management, Jens Lehmann style

"It's weird having your name on a bag of
crisps, but that's football."
**Michael Owen sums up the essence of
the beautiful game**

"If I could be a superhero, I would be
Batman. He's got the least silly tights."
**Worryingly, Paul Robinson seems to have
thought this through...**

"I know it was outside the box, but that should have been a penalty."

Robbie Savage needs to brush up on the laws of the game

"I think I was 5ft 9in at birth."

You've got to feel for Peter Crouch's mum

"I dated a girl from Manchester and she showed me that steak pies and chips are very good."

Cristiano Ronaldo expands his culinary horizons

"When you do bad things, he still wants to kill you, but that is a good thing for a manager."

Cristiano Ronaldo loves Alex Ferguson's mean streak

"If I have a lot of adrenaline in my body, that is helpful because I feel less pain."
Jens Lehmann is a big softie at heart

"When God was handing out brains Jonno decided to have a lie-in. He said to us recently 'There are two suns, aren't there? One here and one abroad.'"
Andrew Johnson reveals Jonathan Greening's Mensa credentials

"Sylvester Stallone isn't Rambo at home. And I'm not the person some people reckon I am."
David Bentley categorically denies being Rocky

"Sometimes it does happen – a child can fight with his father and they are still friends."
Emmanuel Adebayor reflects on his on-field spat with team-mate Nicklas Bendtner

"If this does not change quickly, I will have to go to a witch doctor because there is some kind of wizardry as to why I have not scored."
Carlos Tevez just cannot understand his goal drought

"I'm the kind of player who trains well every day. Do I sound like the teacher's pet?"
Yes, Jamie Carragher, you do

"I got hit in the nose again – and with the size of my nose I'm surprised they didn't have to evacuate the Riverside."
Robbie Savage is a right bleeder

"I don't need to demonstrate that I am the number one in the world. If I am named the best in the world, it won't be a surprise to me."

Cristiano Ronaldo is modesty itself

"That's the second time I've been sent off for celebrating. I'm going to staple my shirt on in future."

Sunderland winger Ross Wallace is prepared to take drastic measures to avoid a yellow card

"At the end of the day, he scored three goals. Other than that, I kept him pretty quiet."

Reading's Michael Duberry had an easy afternoon against Fernando Torres

"I was full of it – I wanted to cuddle everyone I could see."

Jimmy Bullard can't keep his hands to himself after scoring

"When I looked down the leg was lying one way and my ankle was pointing towards Hong Kong – so I knew I was in serious trouble."

Manchester United's Alan Smith knows his geography

"Lampard is a specialist in insulting people very badly."

Jens Lehmann doesn't rate Frank Lampard's swearing prowess

"He's like a second wife."

Benni McCarthy on his special relationship with Jason Roberts

"In football, I don't like to lose."

Andrei Shevchenko has a simple philosophy

"Being a robot, devoid of passion and spirit, is obviously the way forward for the modern-day footballer."
Gary Neville predicts the future

"My dad used to referee me when I was a kid. I remember him booking me – and asking my name."
Coventry's Kevin Kyle is a stranger to his own family

"London is the best city in the world. It's a sea port where hundreds of languages are spoken and where football is played."
Michael Essien fancies a job with the London Tourist Board

"I couldn't tell you what is wrong with my feet but I've just never liked them."
Claudio Pizarro is no foot fetishist

"I will be beautiful again in four or five days."
Cristiano Ronaldo reassures the female population after taking an elbow in the face

"I didn't see the ball. I just saw it going to my right."
Robert Green is selectively blind

"I sometimes put on my kids' Power Rangers outfits to chill out."
Trevor Sinclair likes to unwind

"Goalkeeping is like extreme sports sometimes – you have to let yourself go."
Jens Lehmann on the custodian's art

"I'll take any goal, any time, any place, anywhere – you can call me the Martini striker."
Carlton Cole, cocktail comedian

"Phil Neville once scored against me and, oh my gosh, it was the worst day of my life."
David James is still having nightmares

"Sometimes I dive, sometimes I stand. But I don't care about this. In football you can't stay up all the time."
Didier Drogba is a slave to gravity

"I like to sit around the house and watch TV programmes – but I really like playing football on my Xbox in my boxer shorts."
Cesc Fabregas, kinky gamer

"It was all that leek and potato soup I was brought up on in Wales."
Gary Speed reveals the secrets of his longevity

"Quite simply, it is true that I can be a pig! It is not a lie to say that. Sometimes, I feel I am in the right even when I'm in the wrong."
Thierry Henry reveals his mean streak

"The gaffer wanted me to kiss him but if my missus had seen me kissing him I would have been in trouble."
Crystal Palace's Clinton Morrison keeps his "other half" happy

"I don't enjoy games much. I'm not a skilful player who can have much fun on the pitch."
Javier Mascherano is a miseryguts

"I don't know why he's called me an elephant seal... except for my changing-room party trick where I shuffle along on my stomach and catch fish from the other players."

Trevor Benjamin loves to entertain

"Al Pacino is my favourite actor and I always take my copy of The Godfather trilogy with me. I often put one on safe in the knowledge that if I drop off, it doesn't really matter because I already know the ending."

Kevin Nolan, film buff

"Why should I care if he goes elsewhere? We do not really talk."

Dave Kitson bids a fond farewell to Reading team-mate Steve Sidwell

"I've got a contract with United until 2010, but my future belongs to God."

Cristiano Ronaldo wants to play for the Heaven XI

"I have got big legs and a big backside – it's just the way I am. I will always have a big arse. I can't get rid of that."
David Dunn rules out drastic cosmetic surgery

"I don't want to be modelling G-strings. It's not that good for my image – I'm a footballer not a tart."
Michael Owen, consummate professional

"At the moment I'm just swallowing it all as part of the humiliation but I think – and this is aimed at my dear manager – one shouldn't humiliate players for too long."
Jens Lehmann is fed up with Arsene Wenger

"Tony Blair was on Football Focus the other week and named me as one of his favourite players. My father-in-law phoned me and said 'I've never heard such rubbish!' I voted Lib-Dem last time but I'm Labour again now."
The PM gets Arjan De Zeeuw's vote

"I was fishing and there were some six-year-olds peppering me with songs on the other side of the bank. I trod on my pole and went straight into the water. I crawled out but I had weeds in my hair."
Jimmy Bullard does his Creature From The Black Lagoon impression

"I always had the belief that if you put five men in front of me, I could go past them all."
Cristiano Ronaldo doesn't suffer from modesty

"It is like an addiction, like a drug, you just want more and more of it."
Brett Emerton just loves scoring

"I like the money, but of course teachers should get more than us. I'm not saying footballers should save the environment and change the NHS, but if we portrayed ourselves 15 per cent better then it would help."
Brad Friedel thinks players need to think about their image

"It augurs well that there are so many good young English keepers. Not that I care, I'm Scottish."

Watford's Malky Mackay on team-mate Ben Foster

"Wazza is in the groove. He is a spurter."

Rio Ferdinand on Wayne Rooney

"I can't have a burger without putting on half a stone."

John Hartson worries about his weight

"I'm going to see a witch to see if she can help me score."

Luis Boa Morte seeks magical intervention

"When you see Damien [Duff] coming out of the shower, you'd never believe he's a professional footballer."

What exactly is Didier Drogba trying to say?

"I hate to admit this but I don't even know how to make a cup of tea or coffee. I can boil a kettle for a pot noodle and I've been known to warm up some food in the microwave."

Michael Owen really needs looking after

"I'm about as fast as me Nana!"
Robbie Fowler isn't as fast as he used to be

"Everything in England is shut at 5pm, there is nothing to do, nowhere to go. I just got bored."
Jose Antonio Reyes does his bit for the English Tourist Board...

"We have such terrible weather that often there is nothing to do but watch football and drink beer."
...As does Reading's Dave Kitson

"It will be a difficult couple of days. It's difficult now and it will be difficult tomorrow."
Gary Neville predicts a difficult 48 hours

"I was really surprised when the FA knocked on my doorbell."
Michael Owen. Well, who wouldn't be?

"Not being involved on match days was unbearable, especially the last four games I played in."

James McFadden can't remember when he was on the bench or not

"For as long as you're out injured, it takes twice as long to get back. So I'm looking to be back when I'm about 38."

Harry Kewell is planning a long career

"I don't believe in superstitions. I just do certain things because I'm scared in case something will happen if I don't do them."

Michael Owen fails to grasp the whole "superstitious" concept

"We know we have to score goals, be strong in defence and kill teams in the first half."

William Gallas is nothing if not aggressive

"I'm a big fan of heavy rock music like AC/DC but the lads never let me play it in the dressing room as it's too loud. I love the rock lifestyle and as a kid it was my main ambition to be a rock star. Hopefully I've got the next best thing."

David Bentley reveals his musical frustrations

"I've been training for just over a month now but for the first two weeks of that I couldn't even catch flu."

Goalkeeper Anti Niemi hasn't lost his sense of humour

"Taricco fell over and his feet were in the air. He pushed them out and hit me in the chest on purpose and, as some foreigners do, he was rolling around like a little girl."

Glen Johnson endears himself to the Premiership's imports

"Arsenal are terrible. They can't even kick it over 50 yards. They have to pass it everywhere. It's a joke."
Reading's Marcus Hahnemann has his tongue firmly in his cheek

"I was going to cut my hair the other week and if I had done we'd have lost 1–0, so hooray for afros."
David James hails his expansive barnet

"I never once considered leaving the club. Obviously I had doubts when I wondered if the club would go forward. And that's when you look elsewhere."
Middlesbrough's Stewart Downing is not for turning

PLAYER POWER

"My team-mates call me 'The Thin Andy Fordham' but I'm a better darts player than him."

Robbie Savage fancies his chances on the oche

"I feel I can still do the same job as I did 10 years ago – I've just got a few more wrinkles."

David '100 caps' Beckham spends far too much time in front of the mirror

"Gary Neville is the club captain but has been injured for the best part of a year now and Giggsy's taken on the mantlepiece."

Rio Ferdinand reckons Ryan Giggs has been doing a spot of house clearing

FOOT IN MOUTH

"We feel unbeatable at Ewood Park – even when we play away."
David Bentley loses his bearings

"I've got way too many cars – six here and the others in America. I get up in the morning and decide which one to drive. Most people wouldn't call them classic cars – most people would call them pieces of crap."
Reading's Marcus Hahnemann will never make it as a second-hand car salesman

"I am not going to leave. Never. I am staying here for life."
Thierry Henry stays put at Arsenal – before he signs for Barcelona

"I'm not sure what the disagreement was because those who voted for it were pretty unanimous."
Sir Trevor Brooking needs a dictionary

"Had I not become a footballer, I think I would have been a virgin."
At least Peter Crouch is honest

"He's had three offside decisions, two right, two wrong."
Chris Kamara's argument just doesn't add up

"The fire is always ready, but now it looks as though you're burned on the village green quicker than ever."
Arsene Wenger on football's sacrificial tendencies

"Ten years ago a playmaker could only play when they had the ball. Not now."
Joe Cole on the art of invisible passing

"Crime levels are really high in London. I would not feel comfortable about leaving my wife and children alone at home."
Jens Lehmann endears himself to Londoners

"Arsenal are without doubt the best league in the Premiership."
Sam Allardyce gets it wrong

"Well I'm 28 now and people say you reach your peak at 28, so hopefully I've got my best years ahead of me."

Maybe Kieron Dyer is suffering from premature dementia

"Without being too harsh on David Beckham, he cost us the match."

Ian Wright is a little harsh

"The big thing about Newcastle is there is only Newcastle in Newcastle."

Joey Barton was always top of his geography class

"We're in pole position in second place."

David Healy isn't a natural front-runner

"At the moment we're not playing like a top six side. To be a top six side, you've got to be in the top six."

You can't fault Jamie Scowcroft's logic

"Shocks can happen when you expect them least."

Dundee United's Willo Flood states the obvious

Interviewer: "How do you say screamer in French?"

Wenger: "I'm sorry, I can't speak French any more!"

Arsene Wenger loses the plot

"We will probably have to score more goals than we let in to win games."

Jermaine Jenas has a cunning plan

"If it's anywhere on the pitch apart from inside the 18-yard box, you'd get a penalty."
Chris Kamara wants more spot kicks

"I'm 30 now but back then I was 19... that's seven years ago."
Lee Bowyer mislays four years of his life

"England did nothing in the World Cup, so why are they bringing books out? We've got beat in the quarter-final, here's my book. Who wants to read that? I don't."
Joey Barton isn't big on books

"Most goals go between the posts."
Peter Beagrie is spot on

"Next year I'm sure Arsenal fans would prefer 1–0 draws."
5 Live's Spoony really should know better

"Alex Ferguson is the best manager I've ever had at this level. Well, he's the only manager I've actually had at this level. But he's the best manager I've ever had."

David Beckham trips over his own tongue

"I wouldn't say it's a must-win, but it's definitely a game we need to win."

Peter Crouch definitely doesn't want to lose

"I've worked my nuts off to get here. My groin's a bit sore."

What did Michael Owen expect?

"I've had an interest in racing all my life, or longer really."

Kevin Keegan was a foetal fan of the sport of kings

"Before the game, Naomi Campbell came into our dressing room and saw a few things."

QPR's Dexter Blackstock welcomes catwalk royalty

"That was in the past – we're in the future now."

David Beckham fancies himself as the new Doctor Who

"It's been harder this year. Liverpool have got better, Man United have got better, Arsenal have got better, and Tottenham have joined the quartet of five teams."

Joe Cole was never any good as maths

"He's going to be what? Oh for God's sake! Sir David Beckham? You're having a laugh. He's just a good footballer with a famous bird."

Ian Holloway is Beckham's biggest fan

"Glen Johnson can't help being good-looking – he was born like that."

Harry Redknapp watches his players from a young age

"Andy Johnson has been playing up front on his own with James Beattie all season."

Alan Shearer on Everton's solitary duo

"Jealousy is the weapon of the incompetent and frustrated. It all makes me rewind the cassette of my life and remind me who I was."

Jose Mourinho has an Eric Cantona moment

"I nicked a sheep in Reading once. That was mad."

Maybe John Hartson should be deported Down Under

"Almunia took the criticism and responded with one word – his performance on the pitch."

Arsene Wenger uses five words instead of one

"We have bought two new players. One is younger than the other."

Sven-Goran Eriksson never signs twins

"I consider myself a normal kind of bloke. I get up in the morning and go to the toilet."
Michael Owen provides a little too much insight into his domestic routine

"John Terry is a bloke."
It's impossible to pull the wool over Ray Wilkins' eyes

"If that wasn't a goal, my auntie's my uncle!"
Chris Kamara unwittingly reveals a dark family secret

"We've ended the season on a high – apart from the last game, which we lost."
David Beckham's glass is always half full

"I didn't want to talk to people for three weeks after the defeat. I touched my wife but didn't speak to her."
Martin Jol is an old romantic at heart

"I don't fight about girlfriends. I have lots of them and I'm married."
Portsmouth's Benjani Mwaruwari drops himself right in it

"We are happy with the three points, but it could have been more."
Ryan Giggs is never satisfied

"It's like The Witches of Eastwick. They need Jack Nicholson to come in and sort them right out."
Ian Holloway is glued to Big Brother

"Agbonlahor had a great chance, but really it wasn't a great chance."
Alan Smith can't make his mind up

"I can assure West Ham fans that no stone will be unearthed in our preparation for next week."
Alan Pardew doesn't care about training

"The 2,000 away fans will be unhappy. In fact half of them have gone, there's only 500 left."
Chris Waddle misplaces 500 Man City supporters

"Fourth place is what we're aiming for. We don't want to be second best."
Phil Neville sets his sights high

"I not only like to have the TV and light on to help me sleep, but also a vacuum cleaner. Failing that, a fan or a hairdryer will do. I've ruined so many hairdryers by letting them burn out. So far I haven't set fire to anywhere."

The strange nocturnal habits of Wayne Rooney

"We don't talk about going higher than fifth, we just want to play well. Then with a bit of luck we can go higher than fifth."

Tottenham's Kevin-Prince Boateng forgets himself

"Home advantage is usually an advantage to the home team."

Johnny Giles tells it like it is

"Glenn Roeder will think for a few minutes before making a rash decision."
Steve Stone, with touching faith

"At this level, you cannot defend like that and get away with it. We've defended like that and got away with it today."
Even Steve Bruce thinks he's talking rubbish

"We wanted to keep it quiet, and didn't make an issue of it. We went through the proper channels and hoped it would die a death."
Steve Coppell sensitively plays down death threats to two of his players

"If you're dealing with someone who's only wearing underpants. you're better off giving him some trousers."
Arsene Wenger embarrasses easily

"I have a feeling it's the bottom three who will go down."
Graham Taylor should go with his feelings

"Chelsea have scored in every game this season and they'll need to keep that record up to win today."
Jamie Redknapp knows how to win a match

"It's when Paul Scholes isn't playing that Manchester United miss him."
The genius of ex-Red Devil Arthur Albiston

"Every dog has its day – and today is woof day!"

The one and only Ian Holloway

"This has been our Achilles heel which has been stabbing us in the back all season."

David O'Leary, anatomical genius

"People just looked lost. Too many players looked like fish on trees."

Paul Merson on England's worrying failings

"I had 15 messages after the game. The best one was from my mum, which said, 'Come outside and get some sweets'!"

Manchester City's Nedum Onuoha still has a sweet tooth

"A contract on a piece of paper, saying you want to leave, is like a piece of paper saying you want to leave."
It's all black and white to John Hollins

"I did not have any nerves, although I did go to the toilet just before I came on so there might have been some there."
Theo Walcott conjures up an unsavoury image

"People need to understand what kind of goldfish Wayne Rooney lives in."
Graham Taylor knows something we don't

"My ankle injury's been a real pain in the arse."
Southampton's David Prutton failed his biology GCSE

"Any manager will tell you they'd rather win one and lose two than draw three because you get more points."

Les Ferdinand needs a calculator

"When Jason Koumas is on form, he's the type of player who calls all the strings."

Ian Rush reckons Jason Koumas is something of a rope charmer

"This performance today shows that other teams are going to have to score more goals than us if they want to beat us."

No-one pulls the wool over Darren Bent's eyes

"If I put a cap on, people say, 'It's Peter Crouch with a cap on'."

Peter Crouch is master of disguise

"Unfortunately, we keep kicking ourselves in the foot."
Ray Wilkins knows exactly where the England Under-21 players are going wrong

"When I read a few things, I smell a few coats."
Jose Mourinho should go to the doctor

"I'd like to be a seagull who hasn't been to the toilet for a month and is waiting above Sean Davis' head when he comes out of the shower."
Matt Taylor probably needs counselling

"I listen to 50 Cent, Jay-Z, Stereophonics, Arctic Monkeys, also the musical Oliver – I can sing every tune."
Wayne Rooney reveals too much

"People laughed when David Hasselhoff tried to claim that Baywatch had played a part in bringing peace to the world but I think he had a point."
And you though Moritz Volz just watched it for the swimsuits

"I do not think about the national team too much because footballistically it is not of too much interest."
Arsene Wenger invents a new word

"Leeds is a great club and it's been my home for years, even though I live in Middlesbrough."
Jonathan "Two Homes" Woodgate

"I don't think we threatened the Arse at all today."
Roy Hodgson wanted more from his team at the Emirates

"Cristiano Ronaldo has a left foot, a right foot – the list is endless."
Steve Coppell is simply in awe of the two-footed Man United star

"Jermain [Defoe] is only five foot but he was about eight foot before the game."
Robbie Keane on his incredible shrinking team-mate

"I moisturise daily with Nivea and I regularly use Nivea body lotion."
Freddie Ljungberg is nothing if not moist

"With a team you live in a tunnel and sometimes you have to go down and flirt with hell to see how much you can deal with that, so that you become stronger. But you go quickly to hell and very slowly to heaven."
Bible studies with Arsene Wenger

"I know Rafa well and he will break his own head to find a solution to get the title for Liverpool."
Pepe Reina on his head-banging boss

"I am not happy or unhappy with him."
Arsene Wenger is definitely indifferent

"We were disappointed that we conceded a goal in our dressing room."
Stuart Pearce's defence must be really, really bad...

"I haven't read it and I haven't seen the pictures but it's a fantastic book."
Maybe Sven-Goran Eriksson got the audio version?

"I was still, you know, throwing my clothes out of the pram a little bit."

Joey Barton, childhood stripper

"Why should I? I haven't done anything wrong yet."

Sam Allardyce refuses to resign

"I took a whack on my left ankle, but something told me it was my right."

Maybe Lee Hendrie also got a whack to the head...

"He makes players 10 feet taller."
Rob Lee on Kevin Keegan's surprising abilities

"I'll hire a big chauffeur-driven car so I can take my kids out for a walk."
Florent Malouda misses the point

"Nothing surprises me in football but if I said I was astounded that would be an understatement."
Ray Wilkins does his best to stay calm

"Danny Murphy's been scoring with benders all season."
Bryan Robson casts aspersions

"I'm not that bloke Mystic Meg."
Rio Ferdinand clears up the confusion

"Bingo can be very exciting because you can be waiting for a long time for just one number to make the game complete."
Cristiano "Full House" Ronaldo

"That's what the goals are there for, to keep the ball out."
Lee Dixon gets "goals" and "goalkeepers" confused

"Van Der Sar is one of the best two-footed goalkeepers in the league."
Chris Waddle bestows a backhanded compliment

"Rooney will do anything for you in any position."
Wayne Rooney's keen to please, according to Mark Lawrenson

"Burton just couldn't lose tonight. Except that they did."
Ian Wright forgets the score

"In this day and age you don't see too many footballers with two feet."
Peter Allen is watching a different game to everyone else

"I am a Nigerian and I will remain a Nigerian until the day I die."
Kanu is nothing if not patriotic

"I usually don't have sex. Not on the same day. I say no thanks. I guess that, mentally, I want to keep the feeling in my feet and that's why. I think the feeling sort of disappears out of your feet if you have sex before. I have tried before and my feet felt like concrete when you are supposed to kick the ball."
Freddie Ljungberg likes to save his energy

"I was a bit anxious when I got to the stadium, but in all fairness if hadn't been anxious, I'd have been worried."
Paul Robinson finds it hard to relax

"It's a tough month for Liverpool over the next five or six weeks."

Alan Green needs to check his calendar

"I can't even remember when the Seventies was."

Robbie Keane isn't big on history

"I was both surprised and delighted to take the armband for both legs."

Gary O'Neil reveals his inexperience in the art of captaincy

"The endless coverage of football is made up of the same old clichés. But at the end of the day, that's just football, to be fair."

Moritz Volz, master of the self-fulfilling prophecys

"It is a lot harder when you are 4–1 down than when you are 4–1 up."
Kevin Keegan demonstrates his tactical acumen

"John Terry – he's a great leader. What can I say about him that I didn't say before? He's a great leader."
Chelsea boss Avram Grant does the double

"Some of the Spurs players looked a bit legless."
Gary Lineker questions the Tottenham team's sobriety

"We've got to wake up and smell the roses."
Gary Megson introduces early morning horticulture at Bolton

"We've created some unmissable chances and missed them."

Watford manager Aidy Boothroyd will be having a stern word with his strikers

"It's come off the underside of the errr... thing."

Phil Thompson searches forlornly for the word 'crossbar'

"In a game like that, a draw is better than a win."

Birmingham's James McFadden set his sights low

"Chelsea don't ever run away with a game. Alright, they did win 6–1 last week."

Paul Merson casts his mind back seven days

FOREIGN FIELDS

"Francesco Totti and Alessandro Nesta are like two children pulling a sickie, pretending they have tummy aches to avoid sitting a test in class."

Italy boss Roberto Donadoni isn't convinced his stars are injured

"To leave Madrid is to take a step backwards, or to the side, but it's almost never a step forward."

Gary Lineker can't decide which way to go

"When you score goals you are great. When you don't, you are fat."

Ronaldo definitely isn't bitter

"I wonder what the Italian media will say? They are not accustomed to being nice about me."

Adriano enjoys the press's discomfort

"The Italians aren't the youngest side and may not be able to keep it up for 90 minutes."
Pat Nevin casts aspersions on AC Milan's stamina

"When an Italian tells me it's pasta on the plate I check under the sauce to make sure."
Alex Ferguson does his bit for Anglo-Italian relations

"Being crowned champions this year is a bit like a birth – the more you wait, the more you worry. Let's hope it's not a caesarean."
Lyon boss Gerard Houllier hopes to avoid surgery

"Against Bayern Munich, Maldini didn't make a tackle. That's fantastic. It's an art."
Alex Ferguson doesn't like defenders who actually tackle, apparently

"Bernard [Mendy] is a Ferrari. Although, with this Ferrari, we are missing a driver!"
Raymond Domenech damns with faint praise

"There is a Chinese proverb that says when business drags on, it's like fish – it stinks."
Lyon president Jean-Michel Aulas likes his seafood fresh

"You don't have to have been a horse to be a jockey."

Arrigo Sacchi lifts the lid on the sport of kings

"This squad is effectively a child learning to walk. We stumbled, we will do so again, but our fans are there to hold us up."

Claudio Ranieri hopes to have his Juventus squad up and running soon

"We are not phenomenons, we are gladiators."

Osasuna's Savo Milosevic is a Russell Crowe fan

"You score goals as a kid. Then you grow up stupid and become a goalkeeper."

Gianluigi Buffon on the goalkeeping fraternity

"He's a Spaniard, who has come from Spain."

Phil Neville has got Mikel Arteta's number

"PSV have got a lot of pace up front. They're capable of exposing themselves."

Barry Venison reckons the Dutch are fast flashers

"I have an orgasm when I score a beautiful goal."

Brazilian striker Afonso Alves enjoys his job

"If I walked on water, my accusers would say it is because I can't swim."

German legend Berti Vogts just can't win

"How could they not know? It's not chewing gum, doping is like making love, you need two to do it – the doctor and the athlete."
Michel Platini is a man of the world

"I feel OK. The only difference is in training you have the press – and they want to come back home and sleep with you."
Thierry Henry enjoys an intimate relationship with the media in Barcelona

"Everything's been really positive and smooth. Apart from, obviously, the season."
David Beckham is determined to remain positive after signing for LA Galaxy

"I'm starting to believe that Real Madrid can win the Champions League. No, actually, I don't think they can."
Jamie Redknapp is in two minds

"I always pray before matches. I don't ask for victories, I ask God to protect me from injuries."
Bayern Munich's Ze Roberto looks for divine intervention

"Football is a permanent orgasm."
Claude Le Roy must be a very tired man

"Once Celtic got their equaliser, they played a sort of anti-football."
Frank Rijkaard is unimpressed by the Bhoys

"I don't drive a Skoda. After the game with Rangers in Bratislava, I missed the team bus and a journalist gave me a lift in his old Skoda. I drive a BMW."
Artmedia's Balazs Borbely definitely doesn't drive a Skoda

"The Dutch look like a huge jar of marmalade!"
Barry Davies sums up a nation

"If you see a player who's too confident, you might put him on the bench. If he's still not focused, you might have to sell him."
Gerard Houllier is not a man to be messed with

"Although I am not a vain person, I believe I am the best."
Ronaldinho isn't short of confidence

"The worst thing about playing Chelsea is having to listen to Mourinho afterwards."
Barcelona defender Edmilson won't be buying a Stamford Bridge season ticket

"Marseille needed to score first and that never looked likely once Liverpool had taken the lead."
David Pleat doesn't rate the French side's chances

"I'm a little uncomfortable talking about appearing on a postage stamp in Finland."
Jari Litmanen has an irrational fear of Post Offices

"Montella was as calm as a cucumber there."
Gary Stevens knows something about cucumbers the rest of us don't

"[Owen] Hargreaves is well advised to keep quiet. Otherwise I will get very angry and that will not be good for him."
Bayern Munich boss Uli Hoeness has ways of keeping his players quiet

"The coach is not an idiot!"
Italian legend Giovanni Trapattoni puts the case for the defence

"Romario punched me in the face from behind. You know what? I deserved it."
Diego Simeone has a guilty conscience

"Rosenborg's season has finished and you can't tell me that doesn't have an impact on the mental of their team."
Glenn Hoddle thinks Rosenborg are mad

"Put a shit hanging from a stick in the middle of this passionate, crazy stadium and there are people who will tell you it's a work of art. It's not, it's a shit hanging from a stick."
Real Madrid legend Jorge Valdano doesn't rate Anfield

"I am very happy here in Munich playing for the best team in Europe – that is, unless Real Madrid make Bayern an offer for me."
Brazilian defender Lucio hedges his bets

"I carry on playing and scoring because the new guys are rubbish."
Romario refuses to make way for the next generation

"I am not sure exactly why the winter break started in Germany, but I'm sure it has something to do with the weather."
Owen Hargreaves knows his seasons

"The flight of the ball was really amazing. It was far and high and then it just fell low."
Petr Cech witnesses gravity in action as David Silva scores for Valencia

"People in the street tell me to eat less, but I look in the mirror and I look OK."
Ronaldinho's happy with his figure

"Taking me from behind is something that is not worthy behaviour of a man."
Inter Milan's Nicolas Burdisso wants it up front

"I would say that I am having less sex now that I'm playing in Serie B. There is more to think about in this division."
Gianluigi Buffon just isn't the mood

"When Spain's national anthem came on TV, I sat along and played on the piano."
Real Madrid coach Bernd Schuster tickles the ivories

"Real Madrid need only a draw to qualify for the knockout stages, but a win might not be good enough."
Jim Rosenthal dashes Madrid's hopes

"They're like a bad haircut – lots going forward, nothing at the back."
Robbie Earle dismisses the Barcelona back four

"I stopped trying to be beautiful and thought only of being good."
Ruud van Nistelrooy finally sees sense

"Where I was brought up, they say you have to have received a death certificate before you are declared dead."
At least Roberto Donadoni won't be buried alive

"I was in the doping centre and somebody came in and told me I was in the squad. At first, I thought they were taking the piss out of me."
Italy striker Raffaelle Palladino misses the point

"I hate being kicked when I don't have the ball."
Lionel Messi certainly has a point

"Inzaghi had the number nine, so I went for 99 – nothing to do with ice creams."
Ronaldo clears up the confusion

"Sooner or later I will pose naked to end this discussion of my obesity."
Ronaldo threatens to let it all hang out

"Beckham will be an average cinema actor living in Hollywood."
Real Madrid president Ramon Calderon thinks Goldenballs is changing careers

"You can't shave my head. Winning the title must be celebrated with dignity."
Stuttgart coach Armin Veh doesn't like coiffure celebrations

"I have shaved the hairs of my legs. I put tape around my ankles and it is always a lot of trouble when the hair sticks to the tape. It's much nicer with a massage as well."
Belgian Logan Bailly is a smooth operator

"It is necessary to wear the sandals of humility and not let the win over Manchester United go to our heads."
Vasco Da Gama coach Antonio Lopes favours modest footwear

"At the moment this isn't a group of men, it is a team of little girls."
Palermo president Maurizio Zamparini thinks his side are wimps

"I never think about beating record. I just try to live from Sunday to Sunday."
Luca Toni takes things on a weekly basis

"Over the years, Dida has shown himself to be a very professional and sporting athlete, who even got back up after he was hit by a firework."
AC Milan boss Carlo Ancelotti thinks his keeper is fireproof

"We lost because we didn't win."
Ronaldo is certainly on the ball

"Fiorentina start the second half attacking their fans, just the way they like things."
Ray Wilkins thinks Italian football is getting too violent

"It's better I don't meet the club's officers any more. They don't listen to my suggestions and I'll just get angry and hang them on the wall."
Christian Vieri isn't a man to be messed with

"We can't behave like crocodiles and cry over spilled milk and broken eggs."
Giovanni Trapattoni, reptile expert

"A player can't choose which position he wants to play in. This is not a musical request show."
Bayern Munich coach Ottmar Hitzfeld never watches the X Factor

"Normally when you swap shirts they are soaked in sweat, but Beckham's smelt only of perfume. Either he protects himself against BO or he sweats cologne."
Ronaldo bemoans the former England skipper's lack of odour

"If someone wants to buy Diego, they have to kill me first."
Werder Bremen president Jurgen Born loses his sense of perspective

"After the game against Juventus we received many compliments for our performance, but they scored three goals past us in 15 minutes and put the result beyond doubt."

Livorno coach Giancarlo Camolese's glass is always half full

"You have to win the title here. The fans will not accept failure. If you lose, everybody cries for seven days. If you win, they carry you on their hands."

Fenerbahce's Mateja Kezman on the ups and downs of playing in Turkey

"Barcelona wouldn't scare you if you had to play them. But they've got two world-class players who can destroy you at any given moment."

Jamie Redknapp can't quite make his mind up

NEW
FACES

"It was very nice to enter the locker room. There was a good feeling in there, and I got a good feeling from Kevin Doyle and Stephen Hunt."

Reading new boy Marek Matejovsky is touched by his special welcome

"I don't have any particular celebration – a big smile is all you need."

Tottenham's new striker Dimitar Berbatov on his plans to become the Premiership's smiling assassin

"He has played for nearly every club in the world. It is absolutely amazing how much money he's moved for. He is, himself, a bank!"

Arsenal boss Arsene Wenger on Nicolas Anelka following his move to Chelsea in January 2008

"To get players to come to Plymouth I had to be beat them up and drug them."
Ian Holloway's drastic measures to sign new players

"Sometimes I'd like to have a conversation with a friend in a restaurant without feeling I'm being watched. At this rate I will have to go on holiday to Greenland. But maybe the Eskimos would know me."
Fernando Torres struggles to adapt to life on Merseyside

"On a scale of one to 10, how happy am I? Try 12."
Andrew Johnson is delighted to seal his move to Everton from Crystal Palace

"When I left Fenerbache, I would have liked to join a big club. That has not been possible."
Nicolas Anelka endears himself to Bolton fans in the summer of 2006

"I have not got accustomed to English life.
The food is truly disastrous and it rains all the
time."
Patrice Evra just loves life in Manchester

"If you ask me if I'd pay that amount for any
player then I'd say no. It's an outrage!"
**Luis Figo on his record £37 million
transfer from Barcelona to Real Madrid**

"The English players speak fast and they talk
with an accent. When I'm walking around the
streets of London, people speak so fast that I
don't know what they are saying."
**Chelsea new-boy Michael Ballack
struggles with Cockney rhyming slang**

"I struggled the first few days with breakfast.
Instead of a croissant and cappuccino, I was
faced with eggs."
**Manchester City's Rolando Bianchi just
can't find a bakery**

"Obviously no one has shown him how to use the kitchen. If you want to have pasta, why don't you make it, son?"
Alan Green on Rolando Bianchi's culinary conundrum

"I'm much better for having lived in a garage."
New Bolton signing Gretar Steinsson explains the mechanics of the deal

"The negotiations went very well. The people at Portsmouth know that I will not spend my life at the club. I was able to add a clause to my contract. If I shine, if a really big club wants me, I already know that everything will go well."
Lassana Diarra isn't in it for the long haul

"He says he's a Red, but they all say that when they sign, don't they?"
Steven Gerrard isn't convinced of Craig Bellamy's Anfield credentials

"A new club is like having a new girlfriend – you don't have feelings straight away."
Michael Owen plays hard to get at Newcastle

"I don't feel integrated into English life at all. We cannot speak English, we don't know the culture and we are scared of appearing rude. My two children are in nursery and I didn't realise we should take a cake for the rest of the class on their birthday. In China, we don't do things like that."
Manchester City defender Sun Jihai is homesick

"I can see myself staying at Blackburn for the rest of my career – unless I move to another club."
Benni McCarthy arrives at Ewood Park

"I'm going to find out what any new player is like, what he likes for breakfast and what he has on his chips."
Ian Holloway is a stickler for details

"When we agreed a deal, the manager said 'Why don't we sign it at your wedding'?"
Dunfermline boss Jim Leishman really wanted to sign Stephen Simmons

"During the actual games, it is as though everybody's brains are switched off."
Chelsea winger Florent Malouda gets to grips with English football

"I like to go fishing and diving in the Mediterranean. You can't really do that in Coventry."
Michael Mifsud knows his geography

"I got into football to play football."
**New West Brom signing Luke Moore
probably made the right decision then**

"Samassi Abou don't speak the English
too good."
**Harry Redknapp will get on like a house
on fire with his new signing then**

"Portsmouth have been very good about
this but we've spoken to the player and we
haven't had a response. So David Nugent
can sod off and play for whoever he wants
now."
**Ipswich boss Jim Magilton definitely
isn't bitter**

"I eat what the locals eat. As for fish and
chips, I've never heard of them. What are
they?"
**Middlesbrough new boy Alfonso Alves is
yet to sample the local delicacies**

"Liverpool is special. It is a special team, with special fans and a special city and I am very happy to live in this city and to play for this club."

Fernando Torres tries out his new word

"I must admit I suffered a bit when I first came to England. But then I realised that there was nothing to be intimidated by – everybody had two legs."

Liverpool's Lucas reveals an irrational fear of pirates

"You could buy 10 penthouses up north for the price of something down here. House prices are a joke! They are. It's unbelievable."

Spurs' Jonathan Woodgate isn't impressed by London house prices